FLAVIO RISSATO

Easy guide to operate in the Brazilian real estate market

Buying & Selling, Renting, Financing, Auction and Real Estate Consortium

Historical returns

Real estate funds

Vacation Rentals

Presentation

Hello! I'm Flavio Rissato, civil engineer and federal civil servant.

With my savings as an engineering intern and then a scholarship student at the university, I managed to buy my first property at an auction when I was 23 and I have been active in the Brazilian real estate market ever since, buying real estate through auctions, direct sales, consortium and bank financing, most rented and selling some that generate good opportunities.

What started as a purchase for personal use has become a solid and secure investment medium, as I realized that in the medium and long term, real estate is among the best business opportunities in Brazil.

I am happy that you are reading the book I wrote, which is an easy guide to operate and invest in the Brazilian real estate market, portraying the whole theory and this experience lived over the last few years.

Legal aspects that involve negotiating with real estate will not be addressed, only the various negotiations themselves.

The subjects of the guide range from basic to intermediate and the reading is very pleasant.

At the end of the guide, some appendices are made available, which make a comparison between the historical profitability rates of the Selic (Sistema Especial de Liquidação e Custódia: it is the basic interest rate of Brazil), of the Dollar, of Real Estate, of the IPCA

(Índice Nacional de Preços ao Consumidor Amplo/ Extended National Consumer Price Index: it is the reference index for Brazilian inflation) and shares (variable income), an optimal portfolio analysis with several assets (containing property), a financial analysis of the payment of a housing installment (bank real estate financing) with the rent received for making the property available for lease and a reflection with the options of buying a property in cash or financing it.

To answer any questions or provide any information, the reader can contact me directly through the email flaviorissato@hotmail.com.

As a complementary reading, I recommend accessing the ten volumes I wrote on how to operate in the financial market on the website www.amazon.com, through the series "Easy guide to operating in the financial market" (version for now only in the Portuguese language), a niche I also do investments and which includes some assets in my portfolio in addition to real estate (stocks, options, dollars and government bonds).

I hope you make the most of the knowledge consolidated here!

Summary

- Introduction..6

- The credit market..8

- The purchase of a property: consideration of the economic situation and the interest rate of the economy; consideration of the location of the property and its characteristics, other considerations about the property..24

- The availability (for rental) of a property purchased and the use of specific platforms for rental of properties by season..37

- Comparison between financial investments in real estate and at the Selic rate, in view of inflation..........44

- The real estate auction............................... 51

- Taxes involved in the purchase/sale and rental of a property..60

- Financial Analysis of a Real Estate Consortium.........63

- Notions of Real Estate Investment Funds (FII), Certificates of Real Estate Receivables (CRI) and Real Estate Credit Bills (LCI)...............................73

- Appendix 1: Comparison of historical returns: IBOVESPA x SELIC x REAL ESTATE x IPCA.........76

- Appendix 2: ideal historical percentages for an asset portfolio that contains investments in Selic, Dollar, IPCA, Real Estate and Shares........................81

- <u>Appendix 3</u>: financial analysis of the payment of real estate financing installments with the rent received and whether it is advantageous to finance a property..........90

- <u>Bibliography</u>..101

Introduction

The Real Estate Market is one where buyers and sellers of real estate act, such as land, houses, apartments, commercial rooms, farms and other types of real estate.

As many buyers use the properties acquired for rent, that is, for remuneration for the invested capital, it also gives rise to relations between landlords and tenants.

The participants in this market are individuals and companies (buyers, sellers, landlords or tenants).

Other agents have intermediary roles in the real estate market, such as brokers, auctioneers and real estate credit institutions.

The reasons for someone (individual or legal entity) to acquire a property are diverse, but this type of property, private or public, will always have as main purposes to provide shelter, security, leisure and comfort to its owner/user.

Because of its high value-added asset, doubts about job stability in the country and the lack of credit have a significant impact on the liquidity of negotiations, especially those related to buying and selling.

However, our day-to-day lives are practically all in an immovable property, so there will always be demand in this market, even if retracted when in times of crisis in the economy.

With the Corona virus pandemic, for example, people started using their homes for work in the home office, which caused commercial real estate to become idle and there was a demand for residential properties with more space, especially large apartments, with balconies, and houses.

Therefore, it is realized that there will always be a need for a property, but adjustments in relation to its type should be reviewed over time and with the situation of the economy and other sectors.

This guide, in particular, will comment on real estate operations for the purchase and sale of properties through auctions and bank financing, as well as the maintenance of properties in the portfolio for lease, including the option of making the property available to seasonal guests, on platforms such as Airbnb and Booking.

The focus will be on individual investors, mainly for the issue of real estate credit, but studies of real estate consortium and real estate funds will also be presented.

The credit market

This market makes up, together with the capital, foreign exchange and monetary markets, the financial market.

In banking institutions, there are short (up to 1 year), medium (from 1 to 5 years) and long-term (more than 5 years) credit lines.

The overdraft, credit card and personal loan are examples of short-term lines for individuals and, for legal entities, there are working capital financing.

Financing for vehicles and household appliances may be short or medium term.

While an appliance can cost around R$ 1,000.00 and a popular car around R$ 50,000.00, land, a house or an apartment can cost over R$ 1 million.

Thinking of individuals, the deadlines for payment of such an expensive asset end up passing 30 years, on average, so that the provision of the corresponding real estate financing matches the worker's average salary.

In general, banks require that a maximum of 30% of the total proven income be committed to installments of real estate financing.

This total income is understood as the sum of the possible different salaries, pensions, commissions, rents, consultancies, etc. of the same person as the sum of income from different people and who want to buy the property together (example: husband and wife, brothers or even friends).

In approximate analysis, with the historical average interest rates charged in Brazil and with a term between 360 and 420 months of real estate financing, if a property costs R$ 100 thousand and 20% is input (mostly required by banks), the R$ 80 thousand financed will correspond to a payment of approximately R$ 800.00 and will require a total income of almost R$ 2,700.00/month.

This account is approximate, but provides an idea of the monthly income required according to the real estate balance to be financed or what is possible to finance taking into account the buyer's remuneration.

Detailing the account better, in the historical average, the monthly installment of a real estate loan is about 1% of the financed amount. As the banks allow the maximum monthly installment to be 30% of the total proven monthly income, to reach the necessary income, just divide the value of the real estate installment by 0.30.

The formula for finding the approximate total monthly income (historical average), based on the amount financed, is:

$$\text{MONTHLY INCOME} \approx \text{FUNDED VALUE} \times (0.01/0.30)$$

or

$$\text{MONTHLY INCOME} \approx \text{FUNDED VALUE} \times 0.0333$$

And the formula for knowing the approximate amount (historical average) that can be financed according to the proven total monthly income is:

FINANCED AMOUNT ≈ MONTHLY INCOME x 30

To exemplify, considering a property of R$ 500 thousand, with payment (down payment) of 20%, that is, R$ 100 thousand, with R$ 400 thousand remaining to finance, the total proven monthly income should be approximately:

MONTHLY INCOME ≈ R$ 400 thousand x 0.0333

MONTHLY INCOME ≈ R$ 13,320.00

Or the opposite, if, based on the monthly income of R$ 13,320.00, how much could be financed? The answer is:

FINANCED AMOUNT ≈ R$ 13,320.00 x 30

FINANCED AMOUNT ≈ R$ 400 thousand

And the value of the initial installment (historical average) will be approximately R$ 4,000.00/month, which corresponds to 1% of the outstanding balance.

In Brazil, there is a subsidy in financing rates for individuals in order to promote the purchase of real estate for the purpose of (residential) housing.

In addition, competition between the main banking institutions favors the drop or maintenance of these rates.

The (nominal) interest charged in Brazil for real estate financing, in more recent history, varied between 6.25% per year (plus correction of the outstanding balance by the Reference Rate (T.R.)) and 11.90% per year (+ T.R.), being the minimum practiced in mid 2020/2021.

The Reference Rate/Taxa Referencial (T.R.) was created with the intention of being a basic reference rate of interest to be charged in the month started and not as an index that reflected the inflation of the previous month. At the time it was created (Collor Government, 1991), it represented the average future remuneration for federal and private bonds and, with that, it was expected that the remuneration would mirror the future expectations of falling inflation, trying to eliminate the memory inflationary. T.R. interferes in the values of government bonds, FGTS (Fundo de Garantia do Tempo de Serviço/Guarantee Fund for Time of Service) and the Savings Account, in addition to real estate financing.

FGTS is a fund created with the objective of protecting workers who are dismissed without just cause. The amounts are deposited by the employer and accumulate for the employee about 1 gross salary per year worked.

per year = p.y. from now on

per month = p.m. from now on

In March 2021, when the first version of this book was launched, the minimum nominal rates practiced by the main banking institutions, linked to the TR, were:

Bank	Nominal Rate (p.y.)
Caixa Econômica Federal	6,25%
Bradesco	6,70%
Itaú	6,90%
Santander	6,99%
Banco do Brasil	7,95%
Arithmetic mean	**6,96%**

Source: MelhorTaxa

At that time, the Central Bank of Brazil/Banco Central do Brasil (Bacen) had just raised the basic interest rate of the economy (Selic) by 2.00% p.y. to 2.75% p.y., a rate that had been on the decline since 2015. But this was not immediately reflected in the real estate loan rates practiced by banks, because of competition and because long-term rates "softened".

In order to achieve the minimum rates, the financing term must be short and/or the input must be higher than the minimum required and/or if there must be a "relationship" with the bank.

At Caixa Econômica Federal (CEF) and Santander, for example, you should have a basket of services with about three products including credit card, overdraft, savings and some insurance, in addition to receiving the salary from the bank (or that it be ported there). In CEF, being a public servant, the rates reduce even more. In other banks, it is enough to fit the necessary income conditions.

The highest rates are those known as over-the-counter rates, when the buyer does not purchase any commercial products sold by the bank, such as overdraft, credit card and savings bonds and/or does not have financial investments in the bank.

When considering the capitalization period, the effective interest, in more recent history, was between 6.43% p.y. (+ T.R.) and 12.57% p.y. (+ T.R.), Which would give something close to 9.50% p.y. at midpoint.

Taking into account other rates and the required insurance, the variation in more recent history is between about 7.00% p.y. (+ T.R.) and 13.00% p.y. (+ T.R.), Which are the total effective costs (and these are the ones that must be taken into account when hiring a mortgage).

The maximum payment term is 35 years (420 months) at most banks, provided that the buyer's age plus the contract term is at most 80 years. Therefore, the buyer at the time of contracting would have to be up to 45 years old to obtain financing with the maximum term (35 years).

The amortization system can be the Constant Amortization System/Sistema de Amortização Constante (SAC) or the French System (PRICE), at the customer's discretion.

At SAC, benefits are higher in the beginning and decrease over time. As the debt amortization is greater, an average saving of 10% is saved in relation to the PRICE system.

In the PRICE system, the performance is constant. Its benefit is to provide a much smaller initial installment, which allows the framing of monthly rents that would not be accepted if SAC were adopted. However, if the buyer can support the payment of a larger installment at the beginning of the contract, adopting the SAC, it will be more advantageous for him.

What often makes it impossible to contract through the PRICE system is that, while banks in general finance about 80% of the value of a property and for a period of up to 35 years if SAC is adopted, only 50% of the value of the property is financed and for a period of up to 20 years if the PRICE system is adopted (in some banks).

A simulation on the Caixa Econômica Federal website (www.caixa.gov.br), on 03/24/2021, when the nominal rate was 7.01% p.y. and the 7.25% p.y. effective payment for the purchase of a new residential property in Brasília/DF, for R$ 500 thousand, for payment in 420 months through the SAC system, with a relationship, resulted in a 20% down payment requirement value of the property, that is, R$ 100 thousand, and financing of the balance of R$ 400 thousand in monthly decreasing installments that started at R$ 3,451.04 by the insurer with the best benefit.

In SAC, about 2/3 of the value of initial installments is for payments of fees, insurance and interest, while only approximately 1/3 is amortization.

Therefore, in this simulation, of the provision of R$ 3,451.04, only about R$ 1,150.00 (on average) is amortization. The rest (on average) is almost entirely due to interest, insurance and other fees.

If you choose the PRICE amortization system, the required amount of entry is also 80% of the property value, that is, R$ 100 thousand, but the maximum payment term is 360 months (30 years). The benefit in this case drops to R$ 2,825.26 for the cheapest insurance company.

Over time, not only do rates change. The requirements too. This same simulation, made by the Caixa Econômica Federal website, almost two years ago, when the nominal rate was 8.40% p.y., for the purchase of a new residential property in Brasília/DF, for R$ 500 thousand, for payment in 420 months through the SAC system, with a relationship, resulted in the requirement to enter 20% of the property value, that is, R$ 100 thousand, and to finance the outstanding balance of R$ 400 thousand in decreasing monthly installments that began R$ 3,916.97 by the insurer with the best benefit.

If you opted for the PRICE amortization system, the required down payment amount was 50% of the property value, that is, R$ 250 thousand, and the maximum payment term was 240 months (20 years). The benefit in this case fell to R$ 2,277.50 for the cheapest insurance company.

Real estate installments are adjusted monthly due to the updating of the outstanding balance by the Reference Rate (T.R.).

However, this rate has a very small percentage value historically, even more so in times of controlled inflation.

With the Selic rate below 8.50% p.y., the T.R. is zeroed out. In 2017, it was 0.60% p.y. and, in 2018, it was 0.00% p.y., remaining so until the middle of 2021, since the Selic is at the value of 2.75% p.y. (<8.50% p.y.).

CEF has other financing options, linked to the correction of savings, IPCA or fixed rate. For the same property exemplified previously, the amounts for financing adjusted for savings (Crédito Imobiliário Poupança Caixa/Real Estate Credit Savings Caixa) are:

- nominal rate of 4.84% p.y. and the effective in 4.95% p.y. (for the purchase of a new residential property, in Brasília/DF, for R$ 500 thousand, for payment in 420 months through the SAC system, with relationship)

- Requirement to enter 20% of the property value, that is, R$ 100 thousand;

- financing of the debit balance of R$ 400 thousand in decreasing monthly installments that started at R$ 2,724.84 (Mar/2021) by the insurer with the best benefit.

At the time of the simulation (March 2021), savings were yielding 1.92% p.y. That is, in simple sum of the rates, just to get an idea of the magnitude of its value, the nominal rate of financing for this option would be about 6.76% p.y. and the effective 6.87% p.y.

For the rate adjusted by the IPCA (in the SAC system), the values in March 2021 were 3.88% p.y. (nominal) and 3.95% p.y. (effective), with the initial installment of R$ 2,563.27 (term of 360 months - maximum), for the outstanding balance of R$ 400 thousand.

In 2020, the IPCA closed at 4.52% p.y. That is, in simple sum of the rates, just to get an idea of the magnitude of its value, the nominal rate of financing for this option would be around 8.40% p.y. and the effective of 8.47% p.y.

For fixed financing rate (in SAC system), that is, without any correction, the values in March 2021 were 8.87% p.y. (nominal) and 9.25% p.y. (effective), with the initial installment of R$ 4,229.73 (term of 360 months - maximum), for the outstanding balance of R$ 400 thousand.

There are the same options for the Price System and the maximum values and terms can be consulted in the simulation available by CEF on its website. The other banks present similar products and it is worth consulting them in times of competition between the institutions.

Which is the best option for each person or situation is a very particular decision. You must have a good forecast of the country's economy during the term of the financing to make the best choice, since the values of inflation (IPCA) and the Selic (which impacts on the value of savings) can vary greatly in such a long term, although the products linked to them provide the smallest fixed installments of the total financing rate.

What can be indicated for those who decide to opt for financing with correction linked to the IPCA or savings is that each month amortizes the difference in the installment value for the option of correction by the TR. This can help to reduce the impact of a one-off situation in which inflation triggers, increasing IPCA and Selic.

Example: from the previous data on the purchase of the property, the initial installment for correction by the TR was R$ 3,451.04 (SAC - 420 months) and for the savings correction it was R$ 2,724.84 (SAC - 360 months), which results in a monthly difference of R$ 726.20 that can be amortized over all maturities. Although there is a difference in the term in months (360 x 420), the amount to be amortized would not change much and would be close to that, if the terms were equal. The exact difference can be obtained through the appropriate simulations on the CEF website, leaving here only an idea of the magnitude of amortizations, which would be something slightly above R$ 700.00.

Those who "lock" the rate, in the case of the example, are 8.87% p.y. (nominal) and 9.25% p.y. (effective), with an initial installment of R$ 4,229.73 (SAC - 360 months), it will not be subject to fluctuations in the country's economy over the financing period and will benefit in cases where inflation and the Selic rate increase too much. For this situation, it is worth believing that the economy will not go through good times in most of the contract.

The insurances paid in the real estate financing cover physical damages to the property and the cases of death or permanent disability of the buyer.

So, if any manager comes to offer insurance for the property against this, refuse, since this service is already contracted in the financing.

Also, if it is considered that an eventual death or disability of the buyer settles the outstanding balance, it is not necessary nor to have an extra life insurance for the benefit of heirs for an amount similar to the amount financed, if this type of product is of parallel interest to the client. The difference would be that the heir(s) would receive a low-liquid asset as a "premium", rather than cash.

Of course, over the years, the debit balance decreases and, therefore, the "premium" linked would reduce in the same way with the death or disability of the property buyer. At this point, it is worth considering hiring life insurance that would complement the desired difference, if this type of product is attractive, of course.

In general, about 5% of the installment is for insurance payments. As usual, banks also charge R$ 25.00 per month as a management fee for the financing contract.

Some banks finance expenses with ITBI (Impostos de Transmissão de Bens Imóveis/Taxes on the Transmission of Real Estate) and notary fees, as long as they do not exceed about 5% of the financed amount.

The ITBI (city tax) rate is of the order of 3.5% of the property value (in some municipalities it may be different). Notary fees revolve around R$ 1,500.00 per registered/registered property.

Banks charge fees for legal analysis and property valuation, which, added together, vary between R$ 3,000 to R$ 5,000, and can also be financed.

However, expenses with ITBI, notary, legal analysis and property valuation must be "inside" the maximum amount that can be financed, that is, if the property is worth R$ 500 thousand and can only finance 80% of that (R$ 400 thousand), the debit balance must be less than R$ 400 thousand in an amount that considers these amounts.

Public servants, who have job stability, are the ones who get the lowest rates, but, for those who have FGTS accounts, this balance can be used and, depending on some conditions, you can purchase lines of financing called "pró-cotista"/"pro-quota holders", which have rates even lower than those previously mentioned.

There are developers who build buildings (apartments) or houses and they themselves finance the outstanding balance of the property sold to their customers.

Although the interest rates charged by them are close to those practiced by major commercial banks in Brazil, the correction rates are much higher than the TR, since the Broad National Consumer Price Index (IPCA) is often used updating factor of the outstanding balance.

In addition, the PRICE system is generally adopted and the payment term is a maximum of 20 years.

Financing directly with the developer can be a momentary solution when credit cannot be obtained from a traditional Brazilian banking institution, as it is then possible to port the debit balance.

The lack of credit is not always because of the buyer's income limit or because of some other cadastral restriction. Sometimes it is due to the bank's bureaucracy or even the institution's lack of money.

Between 2015 and 2017, the Caixa Econômica Federal, one of the largest real estate credit grantors in the country, struggled to offer money in the real estate credit modality.

However, some considerations must be made before considering portability.

The main reason is that the total effective cost of the bank to which portability will be made is lower than that of the current contract and that the correction index of the outstanding balance is the same.

In fact, here it is important to highlight that always what must be compared is the total effective cost and never the effective or nominal rates.

Sometimes, a bank has a lower nominal rate, but the insurance charged for it is higher and/or the conditions for maintaining a bank account are more expensive and this increases the total effective cost of the financing contract.

Returning then to the question of contracting a financing directly with the developer thinking of making portability in the future for a traditional credit institution that has a good proposal of total effective cost, some warnings are due:

- if the developer does not have legal conditions in its contract/bylaws to act in a manner equivalent to a financial institution, some banks do not accept portability (it is recommended to research beforehand whether traditional banks consider this developer capable of operating as a financial institution);

- generally the developers adopt a PRICE system and a term of up to 20 years for settlement in their contracts, however, neither the amortization system nor the term can be changed in a portability (therefore, if your debit balance is well above the 50% limited by some banks when adopting the PRICE system, it would not be worth it, as it would have to pay the difference before entering the portability process);

- some traditional banks may not work with the PRICE system at some point;

- the interest rates advertised on the portals of traditional banks are not the same for portability, which are generally the same as over-the-counter rates (it must be confirmed whether the apparently advantageous rate advertised on the bank's website is also applied for portability);

- in portability, banks will charge fees for legal analysis and property valuation, which, together, vary between R$ 3,000 to R$ 5,000; still, there will be the notary fees, which revolve around R$ 1,500.00;

- the reduction in the interest rate, however small, generally has a reasonable impact on the present value of the contract, but it should be analyzed whether this reduction is greater than these bank and notary fees, which, added together, will vary between R$ 4,500.00 to R$ 6,500.00;

- for an outstanding balance of R$ 400 thousand and 360 outstanding installments (SAC), a reduction of 10.00% p.y. to 9.80% p.y. in the total effective rate, for example, it would reduce the present value of the installments falling due by around R$ 6,500.00, therefore, an extra reduction of the order of 0.20% p.y. it would already be worthwhile for a property with these conditions (for other amounts due, it can be simplified to make a proportion in the analysis accounts);

- care must be taken with the extra costs charged by banks that accept portability, such as charging monthly fees for special accounts, which are required by them in order to obtain a cheaper interest rate; therefore, from the example given, if a reduction of at least 0.20% p.y. in the interest rate (from 10.00 p.y. to 9.80% p.y.), but the new bank charges a monthly fee for a special account for an amount higher than what had been paid at the previous credit institution, it might not be worth the portability, as this monthly fee must enter the total effective cost, increasing it (unless the service package is attractive and necessary for the interested party to use it in other demands that, if made separately, would add more than its value).

The purchase of a property

Buying a property without taking into account profitability issues is a personal option for everyone.

Some people, whether physical or legal, choose to own at least the housing property (physical) or that of commercial/industrial activities (legal), without worrying about the issue of valuation, as they only wish to have autonomy to act in the good the way they want, within the legal dictates.

There are also those people who, by family tradition, tend to "collect" real estate, that is, they even have more than their own home, renting the surplus, as they consider it a solid and even profitable investment, according to them.

In the opposite direction, there are individuals or legal entities that consider the purchase of a property an investment that removes the opportunity for gains in other markets considered by them to be more profitable or prevents them from having cash in hand to handle essential activities. Thus, they prefer to rent the property where they live or the factory where they produce and direct any considerable value they have for other purposes.

But after all, who is right (or less wrong)?

There is no answer if someone is right or wrong, as it depends on the beliefs and information that each one has.

Today there are even developers who, instead of building residential buildings to sell the units, are building to rent them, which goes against what commonly happened.

Therefore, what will be shown below is when the real estate market usually shows signs of recovery and appreciation, as well as what to consider in the characteristics of the property and its location when buying it.

Consideration of the economic situation and the interest rate of the economy

The real estate market usually shows signs of recovery when the country's economy is healthy and its level of growth is robust.

Thus, there is a reduction in the unemployment rate and families feel more secure in making long-term financial commitments.

Along with this, the credit market must be heated and with low interest rates for housing financing, because due to the high commercial value of a real estate, it is much more common that its purchase is made through the use of real estate credit than cash payment.

Another factor that has influenced the heating of the real estate market is when the interest rate of the economy (Selic) is low.

Historically, Brazil has always had a Selic rate with values above 15% p.y., which has always benefited fixed income investments, such as Interbank Deposit Certificates/Certificados de Depósito Interbancário (CDI) (≈ Selic) or government bonds.

If we compare the evolution of the variation in the FipeZap, purchase/sale and rental properties indexes (results of a partnership formed between Fipe and the ZAP portal), at https://www.fipe.org.br/pt-br/indices/fipezap#indice-fipezap-historico, between 2012 and 2018, we will see that the CDI has proved to be more advantageous historically (in this period).

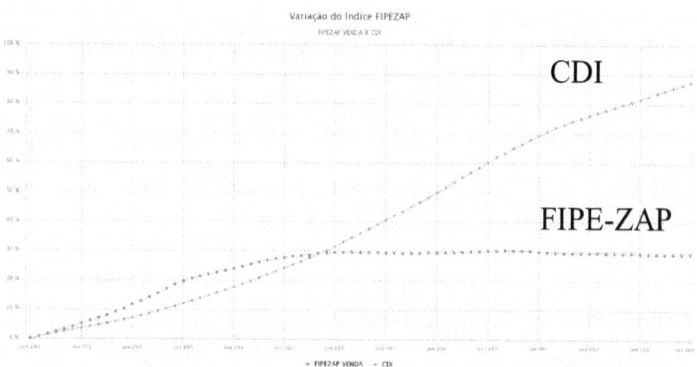

This chart compares the variations of the FipeZap VENDA index (of properties) and the CDI, with reference date Jun/2012.

For the real estate index, the sale prices of all properties were considered, regardless of the number of bedrooms, nationwide.

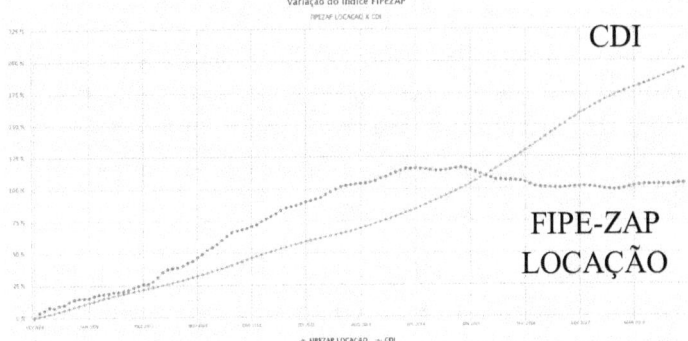

This graph compares the variations of the FipeZap LOCAÇÃO index (of properties) and the CDI, with reference date Feb/2008.

For the real estate index, rental prices for all properties were considered, regardless of the number of bedrooms, nationwide.

As of 2014, Brazil experienced a series of economic crises, which discouraged the market as a whole, including real estate.

Many construction companies stopped launching properties between 2014 and 2019, as they were unable to dispose of their inventories.

After the worst of the crisis and with the credit market on the rise, real estate prices are in a slow recovery, at least following inflation, but have not yet reached satisfactory levels.

The Selic rate, which was 14.25% p.y. in Aug/2016, it stagnated at 6.5% p.y. between 2018 and 2019 and then gradually dropped to the historic minimum level of 2.00% p.y. in the second half of 2020, increasing to

2.75% p.y. in Mar/2021 and tending to close 2021 close to 5.00% p.y. Therefore, investments in CDI have not had the high double-digit returns of the past and investors are considering the increase in the share of real estate in their portfolios, in addition to shares (variable income), since the beginning of 2019.

Furthermore, the fact that there is competition between banks, in addition to Bacen's interventions that "soften" the long-term interest rate curve, will allow the maintenance of good rates of real estate financing for a considerable time, which heats the negotiations with properties.

It is worth noting, however, that, in times when the basic rate of the economy reaches levels close to or above double digits, the real estate market generally slows down, since it is more comfortable and liquid to apply in fixed income and why the taking of credit is impaired for everyone.

Regarding Bacen's interventions, his intervention "calms the nerves" of the medium/long-term investor in times of bad inflation expectations, who usually ask for more premiums in longer interest rates. As long-term interest rates are important for the definition of mortgage rates (which last for about 30 years), Bacen's performance causes these long-term interest rates to fall. This can be accompanied by the negotiation of future interest rate DI contracts on the Brazilian stock exchange, B3 (www.b3.com.br), which is taught in the "Guia fácil para operar no mercado financeiro: Derivativos – Futuros, Termos e Swaps"/"Easy guide to operating in the financial market: Derivatives - Futures, Terms e Swaps" (version for now only in the Portuguese language), in:

https://www.amazon.com.br/dp/B08ZC4WJ6V.

Notions about macroeconomics and nominal and effective interest, mentioned earlier, can also be better evaluated in the "Guia fácil para operar no mercado financeiro: Tópicos sobre Cenários Macroeconômicos"/"Easy guide to operate in the financial market: Topics on Macroeconomic Scenarios" (version for now only in the Portuguese language) and in the "Guia fácil para operar no mercado financeiro: Cálculo Financeiro das Tesourarias – Renda Fixa"/"Easy guide to operate in the financial market: Financial Treasury Calculation - Fixed Income "(Portuguese version for now only), respectively:

https://www.amazon.com.br/dp/B08XW494Y8 and https://www.amazon.com.br/dp/B08ZJXGPFG.

Consideration of the location of the property and its characteristics

Buying a well located property with good conditions of security, comfort and finish can guarantee the buyer success in the event of a possible resale or lease, even in uncertain periods of economy and credit.

However recessive the real estate market may be, there will always be demand for some type of property and, therefore, the best qualified options will have trading liquidity and even chances to generate profits.

Therefore, even if a buyer is thinking of the property only as a good to use, without worrying about its valuation, it is always recommended to look for developments with a minimum of security, leisure, practicality and comfort.

Some characteristics of the surroundings and the property itself may not be valued by some, depending on the age and income groups and/or the location, but in most cases, those properties that meet the list below can be considered good investments.

In relation to the location, the properties that are in the vicinity are more sought after, for example:

- markets, bakeries, schools, hospitals, pharmacies, banks, shopping malls, restaurants, parks and cycle paths;

- public transport (subway, bus), public lighting, pavement and asphalt; and

- policing.

If it is for housing, the ideal is that the property is not located next to these points, but in a few blocks at most, or close to some local direct access road, so that the noise of busy environments does not disturb in moments of rest.

It is very important that the neighborhood is well served by all public utilities, such as water, electricity, residential gas, telephone and data, as well as rainwater and sewage collection.

Properties located in neighborhoods where highways or logistic train lines pass are devalued, because of the noise caused.

If you are close to prostitution points and drugs, non-pacified slums, landfills or gas stations, they are also avoided by buyers in general.

It is very difficult to find a property that meets all these and other possible characteristics, so as really essential items in the vicinity are: public transport, asphalt, sidewalks, well-provided public utilities, policing, basic day-to-day market and that there is not much noise.

Regarding the property itself, what is very important for a good deal is that it has (or is):

- at least one parking space (currently, properties with two or more spaces are more valued);

- elevator and 24 hour doorman, if you are in a building;

- on a high floor, if the street ahead is busy (in this case, from the 6th floor upwards) and there is no double glazing in the windows (double glazing isolates the sound);

- in east/east solar position (this position serves almost all regions in terms of good thermal comfort);

- cheap condominium fee (maximum R$ 10.00/m² of private area);

- good lighting and ventilation, structure (slabs, beams and pillars) and waterproofing in perfect conditions;

- leisure infrastructure (desirable): swimming pool, sauna, gym, toy library, sports court, barbecue area, party room and games room; and

- security cameras and electrified fences.

Some observations on what was previously listed regarding the solar position of the property, the 24h doorman and the technical structural and waterproofing issue need to be made.

- <u>Solar position</u>:

For cold regions, as in the south of Brazil, the ideal is that the face of the property where the most intimate areas are located, such as bedrooms and living rooms, is facing north, as this direction will bring the greatest solar incidence in these points. In hot regions, as long as they are dry, such as the central-west region of Brazil, the face facing south, known as the "cold face" is a good option, because it has less sun during the year. The west (west) face should be avoided in hot regions, because the sun's rays fall lower and lower from mid afternoon to early evening and penetrate almost all the property, leaving it very hot for a good part of the day.

You should avoid having a property facing south in humid regions, otherwise the cabinets and walls may get moldy.

- <u>Ordinance 24h</u>:

The 24-hour concierge is a security issue for the residents of a property, however it is in the labor force that the highest condominium cost is (in this case, it is necessary to hire at least three porters).

However, people have been more concerned with security, even if they have to pay a little more in the condominium fee.

Therefore, this item values the property.

- <u>Technical structural and waterproofing issues</u>:

Structural and waterproofing problems make the purchase of a property unfeasible, because in addition to compromising security, its repairs are very expensive, invasive and sometimes ineffective.

Problems with painting, finishing and old cabinets scare many people, because of the visual impact, but these are the smallest and cheapest problems.

A problem, for example, of infiltration into a baldrame beam (underground beam) of a house (which is the beam that is in contact with the ground) brings many problems, such as mold on the walls, and the most effective solution is to have to excavate and waterproof the beam, which prohibits practically the whole house.

An infiltration into the top slab of a building or the inserts of a facade are also expensive and laborious problems to solve.

However, a structural problem is the most serious, after all it affects the security of the building and its repair either requires expensive and very invasive solutions or requires that everything be redone.

In general, structural problems are not due to designer's calculation errors, but due to execution errors, in which dimensions, positions, quantities and/or types of materials are applied in non-conformity with the project.

Misuse and lack of maintenance can also affect the structure of a building.

For a correct report of any structural problems in a building, a civil engineer should be hired.

A simple assessment that can be carried out is to observe if the property is old and does not have any apparent cracks, it is possibly a solid construction, which has resisted well over time, even with the differential settlements of the foundations already consolidated.

Diagonal cracks that escape from the corners of windows and doors are not necessarily structural problems. They are more linked to the quality of the construction, since it probably was not a concrete beam just below and/or above the window or door that crossed its length on both sides. For old buildings, more than 20 years old, it is acceptable, but for new ones it is not. It may be an indication of total poor quality of the enterprise.

Cracks in the walls correspond, in most cases, to the unevenness of the building on the ground, which happens in the first years after the end of the work, but which stabilizes over time and allows for simple repairs.

Speaking of quality, what is no longer accepted in current developments is the lack of grounding, the execution of which can be checked by the existence of the third hole in the electrical outlets and the corresponding third electrical wire.

Other considerations about the property

There is no right rule for the number of rooms and the types of ideal environments in a property that most value it.

Today there are many people living alone and most couples have only 1 or 2 children, so traditionally, the demand for kitchenettes and 1 and 2 bedroom apartments is great and the launches are mostly to cater to this audience, but this does not prevent the demand for the other developments (with more rooms), considering that there are large families or that want more space.

The pandemic caused by the Corona virus, which put many people to spend most of the day at home, increased the demand for more spacious properties, such as apartments with 3 bedrooms or more, with a balcony, and houses with a backyard.

The questions of the kitchen being open to the living room, or the laundry being isolated or not, or there is a balcony with a barbecue in the apartment, or all rooms have a bathroom (be suites), or the windows go from floor to ceiling are all personal and they do not necessarily add more value to the property, because half the people will like it one way and the other the other way.

In cold regions, the plumbing for hot water in all taps is an example that values the good.

Properties with 1 bedroom tend to have a more expensive square meter (total value/m^2) than one with 2 bedrooms and so on, because the fixed costs of building a smaller property have a greater impact on its sale value than that of a larger one. .

However, small properties are more profitable to rent (in the monthly rent/property value), because the owners are able to pass on a minimum rent amount to tenants due to the fact that the total charge ends up being less than that charged for a larger property and this is accepted by them, even if it is disproportionate to the reduction of the area of the property, since there is a better adaptation to the family budget.

We will then talk about location below.

The availability (for rental) of a property purchased

There are many reasons for a property to be purchased and made available for lease.

One is because the owner lived on the property, acquired a larger one or elsewhere and does not want to dispose of a probable family asset. By renting it, you receive the monthly rent and at the same time you no longer bear the monthly costs of IPTU (Imposto Territorial e Predial Urbano/Territorial and Urban Property Tax) and condominium (if applicable).

There are other people who buy the property as an investment, looking for medium and long-term appreciation and monthly rent payments.

Depending on whether the property is well located, in perfect conditions of use and furnished, it is possible to achieve a profitability (with rent) up to 30% higher than the market average.

For example, to paint, furnish and place cabinets in an apartment of up to R$ 500 thousand, about 10% of its value is spent.

In general, the gross profitability with residential rent for 1 and 2 bedroom apartments is around 0.5% per month (for apartments with more rooms or houses it is approximately 0.4% per month).

If it were not so, it would be better to leave the money in savings, which has a profitability of 0.5% p.m. (per month) when the Selic is higher than 8.50% p.y. With the Selic rate below that amount, savings do not quite yield that, but historically the basic interest rate in Brazil has two digits, which leads to considering a 0.50% p.m. return on savings as a good parameter.

The premium for immobilizing money by buying a property in relation to leaving money in savings, for example, is its appreciation in the long run. Liquidity risk also helps with the expectation of appreciation.

So, for a 1 bedroom apartment, worth R$ 300 thousand, the rent would be about R$ 1.5 thousand. However, if the property is well located, has good furniture (bed, sofa, chairs, etc.) and good appliances and cabinets, all at the cost of up to R$ 30 thousand (10% estimated), you can get something close to R$ 2 thousand/month of rent.

In this case, the gross monthly profitability becomes 0.60% (= 2,000.00/330,000.00), without considering the payment of income tax.

A property valued for rent, in addition to being in a good region of the city, must be painted in light colors, have hydraulic and electrical in perfect working order, have air conditioning, have curtains and lamps in all environments, good cabinets, good finish in general, have at least one parking space (covered and private, preferably), have a lift and 24 hour doorman (if building) and have good furniture if the tenant needs it. Of course, furniture and appliances depreciate over time, so the exemplary profitability of 0.60% would be somewhat compromised with new purchases or necessary repairs, but on average the appliances can last for about 10 years (and have a residual value of 30%) and the furniture can last for more than 20 years without major interventions for changes or repairs.

Old furniture and appliances are not well regarded, so it is recommended to purchase quality items that remain at the forefront for a long time.

The use of specific platforms for rental of properties by season:

The use of the Airbnb (www.airbnb.com.br) and Booking (www.booking.com) platforms has become very common for homeowners who wish to make their apartment or home available for vacation to tourists and travelers in general, in Special.

With the Corona virus pandemic, in which a large number of people became more secluded in their homes, even real estate in the platform user's own city became the option of the so-called "flexcation".

According to the website www.onfly.com.br, "flexcation" is a term that emerged from English, being a mixture of vacation and flexibility. It is a concept or new habit for visitors, which consists of renting houses and chalets for the season as a way of traveling, but without leaving aside social isolation.

Thus, visitors can even maintain their home office activities while enjoying a place with more space, comfort and leisure, alone or with family and/or friends.

At this point, houses with leisure areas (swimming pools) and with backyard space have become good options.

Here, the objective will be to help in the daily pricing of the entire space (not just rooms), taking into account the value of an annual rental contract, turnover, vacancy, accommodation capacity (number of people who can sleeping in the property) and the costs of maintaining the property and all the services necessary for use by visitors.

First of all, in a good rental property for season by Airbnb or Booking there should be no lack of broadband internet with good wifi signal, air conditioning and/or heater, Smart TV or cable TV and the environment must have good furniture, good bedding and bath and be very clean.

Private garage, washing machine and pet acceptance help increase visibility.

24h doorman and security system are also well regarded.

To arrive at the value of a daily rate (ref. 2021), the following premises and average values can be considered (the reader can make the necessary adaptations, according to the real conditions considered by him):

- basic daily rate in annual contract (VB): (0.5% x value of the property)/30;

- broadband internet (INT): R$ 150.00/month (fixed cost);

- condominium (COND): R$ 10.00/m²/month (fixed cost);

- Property Tax (IPTU): R$ 1.5/m²/month (fixed cost);

- water (AGUA): R$ 10.00/person/day (variable cost);

- electric energy (ENERG): R$ 10.00/person/day (variable cost);

- number of people: PERSON (variable);

- number of nights per rental (average) (QTD_DIAR): 3;

- day (s) to prepare the property for each lease (PREP): 1;

- vacancy (VAC): 30% (adopted with statistical basis);

- the daily rate (VD) must be equal to or higher than the amount that would be obtained if the property was rented under an annual contract, for example;

- property value: VI (variable over time);

- area: AREA (fixed).

Thus, we have:

VD = [VB + INT/30 + AREA x (COND + IPTU)/30] x (1 + VAC) x [1 + (PREP)/(PREP + QTD_DIAR)] + PERSON x (WATER + ENERGY)

Since VB = 0.5% x (VI/30), replacing the values for 2021 and making the calculations and simplifications, we have:

$$VD = [(0.5\% \times VI + 150.00 + AREA \times (10 + 1.5))/30] \times (1 + 30\%) \times [1 + (1)/(1 + 3)] + PERSON \times (10.00 + 10.00)$$

$$VD = [0.005 \times VI + 150.00 + 11.5 \times AREA] \times 0.0542 + 20 \times PERSON$$

Assigning values, for example, we have the following for an apartment with 2 bedrooms, of 80m², which will accommodate and will accommodate 4 people, worth R$ 1 million and provide wifi broadband internet:

$$VD = [0.005 \times 1,000,000.00 + 150.00 + 11.5 \times 80] \times 0.0542 + 20 \times 4$$

$$VD = R\$ \ 409.00 \text{ (rounded)}$$

For a 30m² kitchenette that can accommodate 2 people, it is worth R$ 300 thousand and provides broadband internet wifi:

$$VD = [0.005 \times 300,000.00 + 150.00 + 11.5 \times 30] \times 0.0542 + 20 \times 2$$

$$VD = R\$ \ 148.00 \text{ (rounded)}$$

For a 400m² house, which will accommodate and will accommodate 10 people, which is worth R$ 1.5 million and provides broadband internet wifi:

$$VD = [0.005 \times 1.500.000,00 + 150.00 + 11.5 \times 400] \times 0.0542 + 20 \times 10$$

VD = 0.000271 x 1.500.000,00 + 20.00 x 10 + 0.55 x 400 + 5.00;

DV = R$ 864.00 (rounded)

With these bills, a kitchenette has an average daily rate of R$ 74.00 per person. An apartment with 2 bedrooms has an average daily rate of R$ 102.25 per person. And a house has an average daily rate of R$ 86.40 per person.

Thus, on average, one night on Airbnb or Booking, per person, is approximately R$ 88.00 (rounded). As the platforms charge about 3% of the host in relation to the total received, you can increase the daily rate to around R$ 90.00/person, on average.

This can be a base (average) value for the reader to adopt for the daily rate per person for your property. Of course, each one has a different view of the costs and factors adopted, so the previous formula is flexible for the necessary adaptations.

It is also necessary to stipulate a cleaning fee, which in this case is suggested to vary between R$ 100.00 (for small properties) and R$ 300.00 (for large properties).

Comparison between financial investments in real estate and at the Selic rate, in view of inflation

Buying a property as an investment is an operation made by and for a few.

The asset is generally of high added value and requires large disbursements, not to mention that its liquidity is very low.

Sometimes, in times of unemployment and credit difficulties, a property is advertised for sale for more than a year until a potential buyer is found.

Also, if placed by the owner, he must always be ready for any demand from his tenant in order to solve any problem, as the fast and quality service leaves the tenant satisfied and always brings a good return on investment.

In view of all this and having a historically high-paying country in Brazil, it is much more comfortable and safer to apply to a fixed-income security that yields close to 100% CDI, that is, that yields the Selic rate, than in a property.

As already mentioned, people buy real estate for several reasons, but those who think about profitability generally stay out of this market, much because they choose to invest in fixed income, which historically pays high rates, is much safer for short terms and it has high liquidity.

However, with the Selic rate low (2.75% pa, in March/2021), and whether or not it remains above one digit, those potential buyers of real estate that fall into the category of investors are starting to get a little interested more by the real estate market.

Therefore, with the economy recovering, easy credit and low fixed income interest rates, long-term investors begin to acquire real estate as an option for physical assets in the portfolio.

However, as a long-term investment, the appreciation of a property associated with the profitability of its rent equals or exceeds the variation in the Selic rate (historically), as will be shown below.

Using the values obtained from the following links and adopting the base date of Jun/1996, with a value equal to 100 points, we have the table below with the variations of the Fipe Zap, IPCA and Selic indices between Jun/996 and Dec/2018.

Historical Fipe Zap variation until Jun/2015:

https://www.fipe.org.br/pt-br/indices/fipezap/#fipezap-historico

Fipe Zap variation as of Jun/2015:

http://fipezap.zapimoveis.com.br/

Historical IPCA:

https://www.ibge.gov.br/estatisticas/economicas/precos-e-custos/9256-indice-nacional-de-precos-ao-consumidor-amplo.html?=&t=series-historicas

Historical Selic:

https://www.bcb.gov.br/controleinflacao/historicotaxasjuros

DATE	FIPE ZAP	IPCA	SELIC	DATE	FIPE ZAP	IPCA	SELIC
jun/96	100.00	100.00	100.00	dez/07	219.25	206.03	827.90
dez/96	91.67	102.82	109.68	jun/08	239.80	213.54	873.77
jun/97	96.25	107.02	120.99	dez/08	260.70	218.19	931.50
dez/97	108.09	108.19	141.01	jun/09	287.37	223.79	979.92
jun/98	104.31	110.67	158.23	dez/09	316.96	227.60	1.022.74
dez/98	108.78	109.98	179.78	jun/10	348.21	234.62	1.066.58
jun/99	115.58	114.34	207.63	ago/10	362.01	234.74	1.079.49
dez/99	105.35	119.82	226.19	dez/10	393.01	241.05	1.122.03
jun/00	141.71	121.78	247.16	jun/11	448.20	250.37	1.185.61
dez/00	124.90	126.97	266.90	dez/11	498.96	256.72	1.252.66
jun/01	123.25	130.73	286.73	jun/12	537.16	262.68	1.307.27
dez/01	125.62	136.72	312.62	dez/12	577.71	271.71	1.355.91
jun/02	131.00	140.74	339.78	jun/13	612.08	280.27	1.402.60
dez/02	145.55	153.85	371.67	dez/13	658.08	287.77	1.468.38
jun/03	148.81	164.06	415.89	jun/14	687.09	298.55	1.543.94
dez/03	148.81	168.16	459.24	dez/14	706.33	306.21	1.632.38
jun/04	151.61	174.01	493.95	jun/15	721.85	325.11	1.737.12
dez/04	143.15	180.94	532.53	dez/15	721.48	338.89	1.850.23
jun/05	162.38	186.65	580.06	jun/16	721.77	353.86	1.975.77
dez/05	179.91	191.23	633.81	dez/16	724.81	360.20	2.103.83
jun/06	197.73	194.17	693.55	jun/17	725.17	364.47	2.228.97
dez/06	188.21	197.24	741.27	dez/17	723.00	370.82	2.320.16
jun/07	199.62	201.34	783.97	jun/18	721.84	380.47	2.372.75
dez/07	219.25	206.03	827.90	dez/18	721.55	384.71	2,467.47
jun/08	239.80	213.54	873.77	a.p.:	621.55%	284.71%	2,367.47%

a.p. = at period

Disregarding the highly inflationary period in Brazil, which occurred before 1995, which greatly distorts the indices shown here, it is seen that, from 1996 to 2018, the properties appreciated more than 600% (Fipe Zap index) and the Selic appreciated more than 2,300%. Inflation in the period (IPCA) was almost 300%.

The following graphic illustrates the data in the previous table.

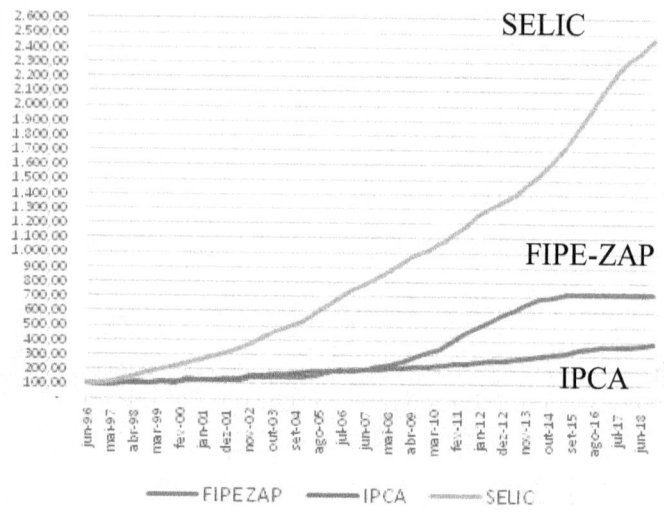

From the previous information, applying R$ 100.00 to properties in Jun/1996, there would have been R$ 721.25 after 270 months, that is, an increase of 621.55% in the period, which corresponds to 0 , 73% am = $(1 + 6.2155)^{1/270} - 1)$.

If R$ 100.00 were applied in the Selic rate in Jun/1996, there would be R$ 2,467.47 after 270 months, that is, an increase of 2,367.47% in the period, which corresponds to 1.19% am = $(1 + 23.6747)^{1/270} - 1)$.

Inflation in the period (IPCA) was 284.71%, which corresponds to 0.50% p.m.

Considering that the profitability of a rented property is on average 0.50% p.m., there would be an extra appreciation of 284.45% in the period = $(1.005^{270} - 1)$.

If the rents received were reinvested in new properties, the total return in the period would be 2,673.98% [= (1 + 6.2155) x (1 + 2.8445) - 1], which would be higher than the Selic rate yield between Jun/1996 and Dec/2018, of 2,367.47%.

The historical monthly profitability of an investment in real estate (considering the rent) is, therefore, 1.23% p.m. (= 1.0073 x 1.0050 - 1), without discounting inflation.

In these examples, tax payments (income tax on profits - IR and property transfer tax - ITBI) or non-receipt of rents due to default or unemployment are not being considered.

What is being shown is that there is a risk in the real estate market and that the maintenance of a property requires a lot of care and time, but, if the property is small, well located, well managed and acquired for the long term, there are good chances of achieve total return at least close to the Selic rate, with this return being enhanced at times when the economy's basic interest rate is low.

With the Corona virus pandemic, even higher value-added properties, with more space, are being well evaluated.

The examples given are also useful for those who buy a property to live in, because the rent that is being neglected to pay on another similar property is considered in the investment's cash flow as an income.

We will now see what the market for real estate auctions in Brazil is like.

The real estate auction

In times of crisis and/or unemployment, people end up paying the creditor bank the housing installments for their financed properties and, thus, they go up for auction.

Generally, auction prices are lower than market prices, between 40% and 60% lower, which can become a great deal for those who bid on them.

The auction of real estate is a simple operation of buying and selling real estate, with the difference that the conditions of the negotiation are not made directly between the parties and there is a commission to the auctioneer.

Interested parties make bids and the winner will be the one who makes the best offer.

Currently, bids are made in person and/or over the internet.

There are extrajudicial auctions, with properties taken by banks granting credit for real estate financing, and there are judicial auctions, in which the property was pledged because of some debt and its sale is made in a judicial process of compliance with the judgment, being the auction. of the good then ratified by a judge of law.

As soon as the property is returned to the bank, up to two auctions can be held.

The first occurs 30 days after its return and the minimum auction value is the market value.

If the property does not receive a bid in the first auction, 15 days later the second auction is held and the discount can reach up to 60% of the market value.

If it is not sold at both auctions, the property is usually offered for direct sale, if it comes from a financial institution.

In judicial auctions and in some extrajudicial auctions, payment is made in cash. In other out-of-court payments, payment can be paid in up to 24 months or financed in up to 35 years, depending on which bank is the property available for auction. Santander, for example, usually provides real estate financing for the properties it repossessed and auctioned.

The auctioneer's commission is usually 5% of the auctioned value and the deposit paid for properties to be paid in installments is about 10% of the auctioned value (the deposit is then deducted from the outstanding balance).

It is known that auctioned properties are offered at a minimum bid with discounts in the order of 10%, 20%, 30% or even 60% in relation to the market value, but the purchase of a property at auction is only worthwhile (in a vision of profit with the subsequent sale) if the final discount is on average at least 35%.

There are several taxes, fees and other costs linked to a property that is intended to be bought at auction and then to be sold.

That is why it is first important to make sure that the discount advertised in the auction for the minimum bid is real, that is, one must research the prices of a similar property in the advertisements of websites and newspapers and have an idea of its market value.

If you cannot find a property similar to the sale, it is recommended to talk to a real estate agent who knows the region for a better evaluation.

Knowing the market value of the property and its minimum bid in the auction, the following analyzes must be made - based on a property (occupied), valued at R$ 143 thousand and which is in the auction notice with a minimum bid of R$ 96 thousand, for example (this was a real case found on the Caixa Econômica Federal website for a house in Brasília/DF).

In this case, there is an initial discount of around 33%, which may or may not be effective, depending on the dispute in the auction. It is, therefore, just a reference of the maximum discount that can be obtained with this property.

The taxes, fees and costs (approximate) in the purchase of a property at auction that you intend to sell later are, in 2021:

- Auctioneer's commission (5% of the auctioned value);

- ITBI and notary fees (5% of the auctioned value);

- Possible renovation of the property (5% of the market value);

- Brokerage when selling (3% of the market value);

- Attorneys' fees in the event of a lawsuit to remove the resident from the occupied property (R$ 10,000);

- Loss of profits until the sale (0.5% p.m. in relation to the market value);

- IPTU and delayed condominiums, if any; and

- Income Tax on the profit from the sale (15% of the difference between the sale price and the purchase price, less sales commissions and the auctioneer);

Considering that, because the property is occupied, there is no dispute in the bids and the property is sold for the minimum amount (R$ 96 thousand), that an action of withdrawal of the resident lasts 5 months, that the property will be announced to the sale for another 5 months (in a total of 10 months since the purchase), that there is R$ 3 thousand in IPTU and condominium debts and that the real estate market does not appreciate in the next 12 months, we have the following table.

Value purchased	R$	96,000.00
		-32.87%
Sale Price	R$	143,000.00
(-) Auctioneer's commission (5% of the auctioned value)	-R$	4,800.00
(-) ITBI and notary fees (5% of the auctioned value)	-R$	4,800.00
(-) Renovation of the property (5% of the market value)	-R$	7,150.00
(-) Brokerage at the time of sale (3% of the market value)	-R$	4,290.00
(-) Attorney fees for legal action for removal of resident of occupied property (R$ 10,000)	-R$	10,000.00

(-) Loss of profits until sale (0.5% per month x 10 months) - percentage in relation to market value	-R$	7,150.00
(-) IPTU and delayed condominiums	-R$	3,000.00
(=) Amount before income tax	R$	101,810.00
(-) Income tax on profit from sale (15% of the difference between the sale price and the purchase price, less the sales commission and the auctioneer)	-R$	5,686.50
(=) Final value of the property	R$	96,123.50
		-32.78%
Net Profit in the period (final property value - auctioned value)	R$	123.50
		0.13%

Generally, occupied properties tend to have IPTU and condominium debts, especially if the resident is the former owner.

Still, they almost always need renovations, however punctual they may be (the resident usually takes them to the doors with him, if he is the former owner!).

For the removal of the resident, a lawsuit is necessary and this entails costs in the order of R$ 10,000 (in 2021).

For the example given, buying a property occupied at an auction, with a discount of about 30%, the net profit from the purchase and sale operation was practically equal to zero, which is not worth it in view of the high bureaucracy and the high values and terms involved.

The period involving the payment date and the sale date can last an average of 10 months, according to the example. Therefore, in order to gain at least the Selic rate variation (2.75% p.y.) in this period, the profit should be 2.29% a.p. = $(1.0275^{10/12} - 1)$. This profit would be obtained if the property had been purchased for something close to R$ 93 thousand, that is, with a discount of approximately 35%.

With this information, it is clear that the minimum purchase price at auction for a occupied property is at least 35% off the market.

This discount is the average granted by financial institutions. Discounts greater than 35% in relation to the market price make the acquisition at auction more attractive, if you think about reselling the property next.

For those who are thinking of buying the property to live in, the discount to be considered is much smaller and comes in the order of 23% (closing value equal to R$ 110 thousand for this example), because they would only be considered the auctioneer's commission, the costs with the renovation of the property, the payment of attorney fees and of the IPTUs and delayed condominiums and the lost profits until the vacancy and renovation of the property.

In other words, this 23% is the minimum discount to be earned on a purchase via real estate auction. Any discount of less than 23% removes interest in this mode of acquisition.

In view of all these data, which are not difficult to obtain by people, the big draw when buying a property at auction is when the property is advertised as occupied and is actually empty.

Most people, when they lose their property because they are unable to pay housing benefits in times of crisis and unemployment, end up leaving it during the process of repossession by the financial institution without communicating it.

Therefore, it is very important that the person interested in an auction property should go to your location and try to talk to the liquidator, or the porter, or the neighbors to confirm that the property is still occupied.

If the resident is still living in the property, it would be interesting to try to talk to him also to find out about his expectations regarding the process of repossessing the property and if he intends to leave it soon.

Visiting the location of the property advertised at auction is very important not only to know if the resident is still there, but also to see how the street, the neighborhood, the position of the property is in case of being in a building (if east, west) etc.), if there is a 24-hour concierge, if the facade needs repairs that will require extra costs and long intervention and if there are overdue condominiums and the corresponding total, if the property is in a building (in this case, talk to the supervisor or the administration of the condominium is indicated to obtain this information).

The pending issues with IPTU can be checked on the internet through the registration of the property, which is usually informed in the auction notices.

If a property is sold at auction, but the resident and until then owner obtains a court injunction that annuls its sale, all amounts paid, as a commission to the auctioneer and a business signal to the bank, are promptly returned. There is no reason to worry about that.

Returning to the subject of whether it is advantageous to have a deal at auction over a property that is informed as occupied, but which is actually empty, we have the following:

- when the banking institution finds occupation in the repossessed property, in general, if the second auction occurs, the discount given for the initial minimum bid is greater than 35%, reaching up to 60%;

- properties informed as occupied in auction notices are generally despised by the participants, due to all the risk and cost involved in trying to remove the resident from the property, which has to be judicial in most cases;

- as the possible occupation discourages the purchase, the dispute for lots informed as occupied is low, which allows the auction many times for the minimum value or just above that.

Using the previous example and considering that the property informed as occupied is in fact unoccupied, but will be auctioned off by the minimum bid of R$ 96 thousand due to the lack of interest of the uninformed, there are no costs with attorney fees and the lost profits will only occur for 5 months, which would be the average time to renovate the property (if the intervention is small) and find a buyer.

Thus, the table with the summary of gains and costs is as follows.

Value purchased	R$	96,000.00
		-32.87%
Sale Price	R$	143,000.00
(-) Auctioneer's commission (5% of the auctioned value)	-R$	4,800.00
(-) ITBI and notary fees (5% of the auctioned value)	-R$	4,800.00
(-) Renovation of the property (5% of the market value)	-R$	7,150.00
(-) Brokerage at the time of sale (3% of the market value)	-R$	4,290.00
(-) Attorney fees for legal action for removal of resident of occupied property (R$ 10,000)		
(-) Loss of profits until sale (0.5% per month x 5 months) - percentage in relation to market value	-R$	3,575.00
(-) IPTU and delayed condominiums	-R$	3,000.00
(=) Amount before income tax	R$	115,385.00
(-) Income tax on profit from sale (15% of the difference between the sale price and the purchase price, less the sales commission and the auctioneer)	-R$	5,686.50
(=) Final value of the property	R$	109,698.50
		-23.29%
Net Profit in the period (final property value - auctioned value)	R$	13.698.50
		14.27%

A profit of 14.27% in five months corresponds to an annual profitability of 37.73% (= $1.1427^{12/5} - 1$), which is very attractive, especially when the fixed income remuneration is low, around 2.75% pa

It is clear that this profitability will only be obtained if the property is sold in five months. If this takes a year, profitability will be 14.27%, which is still interesting at the moment.

The taxes involved in the purchase/sale and lease of a property

In real estate transactions, the impacts that taxes have on the final profitability of the operation must be considered.

The ITBI (Imposto de Transmissão de Bens Imóveis Inter Vivos/Tax on Transmission of Real Estate between living people), paid to the municipality, has a rate of around 3.5%, applied on the purchase price (or whichever is greater when considering the price estimated by the city). For a property of R$ 300 thousand, for example, the ITBI would be R$ 10,500.00, which impacts the cost of acquisition when the focus is profitability.

Income tax (IR) must be paid on the proceeds from the sale and on the rent received.

For individuals, the income tax rate is 15% on the profit on the sale of a property.

This profit is the basis for calculating the tax and is obtained by the difference between the sale price and the purchase price, less the commission paid to the broker.

There is also a reduction on this basis by the factor $FR = 1/1.0035^m$ (of article 40, § 1, II, of Federal Brazilian Law 11.196/2005) for properties acquired after 2005, where m = number of months passed between the purchase and the sale.

For example, if a property was purchased for R$ 300 thousand five years ago (60 months) and was sold for R$

350 thousand, with a 3% commission, the IR to be paid will be informed below.

Profit = 350,000 - 300,000 - 350,000 x 3% = 39,500.00

FR = $1/1.0035^{60}$ = 0.810881 (reducer)

Calculation basis = 0.810881 x 39,500 = 32,029.82

IR = 15% x 32,029.82 = 4,804.47

This amount must be collected through DARF (Documento de Arrecadação de Receitas Federais/Federal Revenue Collection Document).

In relation to rents, if the owner is an individual and already receives a salary above R$ 4,664.68/month, the rate will be 27.5% on the monthly rent.

For example, if the rent is R$ 1,500.00/month for a property that cost R$ 300,000.00, the income tax will be R$ 412.50/month, which greatly reduces the net profitability of the operation. If the property is being managed by a real estate company, about 8% per month is charged as an administration fee (on the rental amount), which would result in R$ 120.00/month. The net profitability with the rent would thus be 0.32% p.m. [= (1,500.00 - 412.50 - 120.00)/300,000.00].

In fact, the most correct calculation is to discount the payment to the real estate company to arrive at the basis for calculating the IR. Thus, the IR would be R$ 379.50 [= (1,500.00 - 120.00) x 0.275]. The owner would be left with R$ 1,000.00 (= 1,500.00 - 120.00 - 379.50).

To earn net 0.50% per month, considering the payment of the income tax and the administration fee of the real estate, the rent should be 0.78% per month in relation to the value of the property, which could be achieved only if it were a small property, well located, with good finish, good furniture and good appliances.

For this gross profitability, we have the following, for a property worth R$ 300,000.00:

Rent = 0.78% x 300,000 = R$ 2,340.00;

Management fee (real estate) = 8% x 2,340 = R$ 187.20;

Income Tax = 27.5% x (2,340 - 187.20) = R$ 592.02

Net income = 2,340 - 187,20 - 592,02 = R$ 1560.78 ($\approx$ 0.5% of R$ 300 thousand).

Still, this gross profitability (0.78% p.m.) is difficult to obtain, even for a property with these characteristics. If the owner wants to receive a little more, he could try to manage the lease of the property himself.

The advantages of having a property available for rent, in terms of investment, lies in the set of rent received + valuation of the property over time. That is why investing in real estate requires the immobilization of money in the medium/long term. For those who plan to need the money in the short term and still want to invest in real estate, the best option would be to buy funds from this sector.

Financial Analysis of a Real Estate Consortium

Here you will be shown a financial analysis of a real estate consortium. Therefore, the personal option of choosing a real estate consortium instead of real estate financing, or vice versa, for any other reason, is the decision of each one.

The analysis will be made for the option to bid and finish the letter of credit at the beginning of the consortium, because the option to wait for contemplation via the draw is a matter of luck and here, in a technical analysis, it cannot be considered, as the comparison with real estate financing would be unfeasible. **The results show that the bid cannot exceed about 42.5% of the total paid in the consortium (for the most pessimistic view in relation to the future real estate market).**

The real estate consortium is basically an association of people who come together for each month to contribute a portion that will add up and accumulate to the total letter of credit to be acquired in the use of the purchase of a property and people who will already be able to take advantage of the letter of credit are drawn every month. There is no interest, but an administration fee is paid, the percentage of which is applied to the value of each letter of credit. The installments are corrected by the National Construction Cost Index (Índice Nacional de Custo da Construção – INCC), but the value of the letter of credit is adjusted by the same factor.

Contemplation by drawing lots at the beginning of payments would be the "best of all worlds", because if we consider only the application of the administration fee, which is about 20%, in a period of about 200 months, for example, it would be as if monthly interest was approximately 0.19% per month!

It has been commented on previous pages that the effective monthly interest of a real estate financing, in more recent history, is close to 0.76% p.m. (or 9.50% p.y.), in midpoint.

The two biggest "drawbacks" of a real estate consortium is that the participant who waits for the draw could be investing the value of the monthly installments in another investment that would correct the amount and that, when placing a bid to acquire the letter of credit in advance, this amount that the participant saved until then, due to his effort, is taxed in the same way by the administration fee of the consortium.

Consulting the real estate consortium options on the market, he is faced with a value of R$ 248,184.00, in 156 installments of R$ 1,901.15. This is the result of a 19.50% administration fee. It will be considered in the calculations.

The following analysis admits that the bid will be sufficient to win the letter of credit at the beginning of the consortium, as this is the only way to compare it with real estate financing, in which the interested party already has the property available after contracting. In this case, the possible rents that will be received by the new property or the fact that the interested party fails to pay it when moving to the property will also be considered.

As a rule, after a contemplated bid, the number of installments is reduced and the installment amount is maintained.

In the first analysis, it will be evaluated what would have to be the percentage of the bid in relation to the total value of the consortium (value of the letter + administration fee) so that the monthly fee would be equivalent to a monthly fee of 0.76% per month (or 9,50% p.y.), which is the average effective rate for real estate financing, in more recent history.

So, we have the following spreadsheet:

LETTER AMOUNT (PROPERTY):	248,184.00	
ADMINISTRATION FEE:	19.50%	
TOTAL AMOUNT OF THE LETTER (WITH ADMINISTRATION FEE):	296,579.88	
INSTALLMENT (QUANTITY OF MONTHS):	156	
AMOUNT OF MONTHLY INSTALLMENT:	1,901.15	
PERCENTAGE OF BID:	41.6%	(in relation to the total)
BID AMOUNT:	123,377.23	
NEW TERM (MONTHS) AFTER LAUNCH:	91	(term reduces and the amount of the installment remains)
NET AMOUNT RECEIVED FROM THE LETTER:	124,806.77	
CASH FLOW CONSORTIUM:		
DISBURSEMENT	123,377.23	
AMOUNT OF THE LETTER (OR PROPERTY):	248,184.00	
INITIAL NET GAIN:	124,806.77	
VALUE OF MONTHLY INSTALLMENT:	1,901.15	
MONTHLY OPERATION RATE:	0.76%	

A real estate financing would have the following conditions with an average rate of 9.50% p.y.:

CASH FLOW FUNDING:	
PROPERTY VALUE:	248,184.00
PERCENTAGE OF ENTRY:	20%
ENTRY AMOUNT:	49,636.80
FINANCED AMOUNT:	198,547.20
PAYMENT (PRICE):	R$ 3,027.11
ANNUAL REFERENCE FEE (CET - FINANCING):	9.50%
MONTHLY REFERENCE RATE (FINANCING):	0.76%

From the consortium table, using Excel's "Reach Goal", so that the monthly fee for the operation would equal the total effective cost/custo efetivo total (CET) of an average real estate loan (0.76% per month), the percentage of the total consortium in bid should be 41.6%. **This is almost 50% of the letter of credit. Above that, disregarding the internal rate of return, bureaucracy and other personal options, it would be more feasible to opt for real estate financing.**

The problem in this analysis lies in the fact that the "entry" (bid) of a consortium is about 50% of the value of the letter of credit (or of the property), while in financing this is only 20%. Then, in a second analysis, a comparison of the internal rates of return (IRR) – taxa interna de retorno (TIR) – of the two options will be seen below in order to consider what is disbursed at the beginning and what is paid monthly.

For the calculation of the internal rate of return (IRR), the cash flow of the operation must be complete. Therefore, it is necessary to estimate the value of the property during the payment period. The gross profitability of 1.23% will be adopted (appreciation of the price of the property + reinvested rent), which was presented in the previous pages.

This is necessary because, in the previous analysis, the initial disbursement in the consortium is higher, although the installment is lower in relation to what happens for real estate financing.

The result of the IRR analysis of the two options (consortium and financing) shows that, considering the appreciation of 1.23% per month for properties, so that the rates of return are equal, the maximum bid in relation to the total (letter of credit + management fee) must equal 31.5% (or 38% of the letter of credit). The IRR in this case is around 18.85% p.y. for both options.

The following tables show this.

LETTER AMOUNT (PROPERTY):	248,184.00	
ADMINISTRATION FEE:	19.50%	
TOTAL AMOUNT OF THE LETTER (WITH ADMINISTRATION FEE):	296,579.88	
INSTALLMENT (QUANTITY OF MONTHS):	156	
AMOUNT OF MONTHLY INSTALLMENT:	1,901.15	
PERCENTAGE OF BID:	31.5%	(in relation to the total)
BID AMOUNT:	93,422.66	
NEW TERM (MONTHS) AFTER LAUNCH:	107	(term reduces and the amount of the installment remains)
NET AMOUNT RECEIVED FROM THE LETTER:	154,761.34	
CASH FLOW CONSORTIUM:		
DISBURSEMENT	93,422.66	
AMOUNT OF THE LETTER (OR PROPERTY):	248,184.00	
	916,471.22	
INITIAL NET GAIN:	154,761.34	
VALUE OF MONTHLY INSTALLMENT:	1,901.15	
MONTHLY OPERATION RATE:	0.53%	
ANNUAL OPERATION RATE:	6.56%	
CASH FLOW FUNDING:		
PROPERTY VALUE:	248,184.00	
PERCENTAGE OF ENTRY:	20%	
ENTRY AMOUNT:	49,636.80	
FINANCED AMOUNT:	198,547.20	
PAYMENT (PRICE):	R$2,719.12	
PROPERTY VALUE AFTER PAYMENT:	916,471.22	
ANNUAL REFERENCE FEE (CET - FINANCING):	9.50%	
MONTHLY REFERENCE FEE (FINANCING):	0.76%	
MONTHLY HISTORICAL VARIATION ADOPTED (PROPERTIES)	1.23%	

If only the appreciation of property prices (0.73% p.m.) is considered, conservatively, the maximum bid should be 42.5% of the total (letter of credit + management fee) or about 51% of the letter of credit. The IRR in this case is around 8.92% p.y. for both options.

The following tables show this.

LETTER AMOUNT (PROPERTY):	248,184.00
ADMINISTRATION FEE:	19.50%
TOTAL AMOUNT OF THE LETTER (WITH ADMINISTRATION FEE):	296,579.88
INSTALLMENT (QUANTITY OF MONTHS):	156
AMOUNT OF MONTHLY INSTALLMENT:	1,901.15
PERCENTAGE OF BID:	42.5% (in relation to the total)
BID AMOUNT:	126,046.45
NEW TERM (MONTHS) AFTER LAUNCH:	90 (term reduces and the amount of the installment remains)
NET AMOUNT RECEIVED FROM THE LETTER:	122,137.55
CASH FLOW CONSORTIUM:	
DISBURSEMENT	126,046.45
AMOUNT OF THE LETTER (OR PROPERTY):	248,184.00
	476,563.95
INITIAL NET GAIN:	122,137.55
VALUE OF MONTHLY INSTALLMENT:	1,901.15
MONTHLY OPERATION RATE:	0.78%
ANNUAL OPERATION RATE:	9.82%
CASH FLOW FUNDING:	
PROPERTY VALUE:	248,184.00
PERCENTAGE OF ENTRY:	20%
ENTRY AMOUNT:	49,636.80
FINANCED AMOUNT:	198,547.20
PAYMENT (PRICE):	R$ 3,060.05
PROPERTY VALUE AFTER PAYMENT:	476,563.95
ANNUAL REFERENCE FEE (CET - FINANCING):	9.50%
MONTHLY REFERENCE FEE (FINANCING):	0.76%
MONTHLY HISTORICAL VARIATION ADOPTED (PROPERTIES)	0.73%

In conclusion, in comparison with a real estate financing, considering only the financial flow of the operations, the maximum bid to be given in a real estate consortium for immediate consideration of the letter of credit is 31.5% (of the value of the letter + management fee) by adopting as profitability the historical valuation of properties added to the profitability with rent reapplied (or by the fact of not paying rent), which is 1.23% per month.

If there is not much optimism regarding the profitability with properties and if, for example, only the historical variation of their prices (0.73% per month) is considered, leaving aside the rent portion, conservatively, the maximum bid is 42.5% in relation to the total (letter of credit + management fee).

In magnitude, rounding the percentages, we can say that the maximum bid is in an interval of the order of 30% to 40% of the total (letter of credit + management fee), depending on the expectation of appreciation of the properties that the interested party considers. If you are optimistic, do not bid much higher than 31.5% and, if you are not so optimistic, do not bid much above 42.5%. If time goes by and the investor is not contemplated at the beginning, these percentages must be revised.

Real Estate Investment Funds (FII), Certificates of Real Estate Receivables (CRI) or Real Estate Letters of Credit (LCI)

One way to invest in real estate and with a little more liquidity is through the purchase of shares in **Real Estate Investment Funds (Fundos de Investimento Imobiliário: FII)** or **Certificates of Real Estate Receivables (Certificados de Recebíveis Imobiliários: CRI)** or **Real Estate Letters of Credit (Letras de Crédito Imobiliário: LCI)**.

The focus in this guide is on the purchase and direct management of the real asset, soon the characteristics of these types of investments will be briefly explained.

While FIIs are traded through a home broker, as variable income, CRIs and LCIs are fixed income investments.

In FIIs, investors come together to buy or build real estate together (through quotas) (there is ownership over a fraction of the good) and pass their administration on to a professional manager.

There are also real estate funds that invest in shares of other funds in the sector and/or in LCIs and CRIs.

The following link contains the list of FIIs listed on B3 (Brazilian stock exchange).

http://www.b3.com.br/pt_br/produtos-e-servicos/negociacao/renda-variavel/fundos-de-investimentos/fii/fiis-listados/

The main earnings of the shareholders of an FII are through the apportionment of the rents received for making the venture (or units) available for lease.

The valuation of quotas and when the properties are sold and the fund is dissolved are also forms of gains through the FIIs, as in the negotiation of shares of companies on the stock exchanges.

The risks of an FII are the common ones related to the purchase and rental of a property, such as devaluation of the project, default of the tenants and when the properties are empty (there is no rent receipt and there are fixed costs with condominium and property tax).

For example, with the pandemic caused by the Corona virus, which started in 2020, several shopping centers had to close their doors, so funds related to space rental in shopping centers and corporate and/or commercial rooms had a certain loss.

The constant restructuring of banking institutions, with the closing of several branches, also negatively impact the profitability of funds tied to leasing for this type of legal entity, something that until then was considered one of the best options in this type of application, since the gains net surpassed 0.60% per month (as seen in this guide, on average, gains on residential leasing are between 0.40% per month and 0.50% per month).

CRIs and LCIs, on the other hand, are fixed income securities in which the invested capital is adjusted, adjusted by a market index plus a defined rate at the time of acquisition.

LCIs are issued by banks/financial institutions and remuneration occurs when the security is settled.

CRIs are issued by real estate credit securitization companies and earnings are received by month, quarter, semester or year.

Acquiring a CRI is like buying rental and financing debt securities, for example.

Therefore, there is a credit risk if there is a default in the receipts from the securitization company.

In all cases, the backing of physical properties serves as a guarantee in situations of non-payment.

There is exemption from IR for FIIs, CRIs and LCIs, except for any profit from the valuation when a FII share is sold (there is a 20% tax on the gain).

Annex 1: Comparison of historical profitability: IBOVESPA x SELIC x REAL ESTATE x IPCA

As shown in this guide, the valuation of a property associated with the profitability of its rent can equal or exceed the variation of the Selic rate (historically), in the long run.

The graph below shows the variation in properties for sales only. The consideration of the rent, which makes the total profitability of the properties surpass the Selic historically, will be explained below.

Here, the historical variation of the IBOVESPA (variable income) will be included in the comparison.

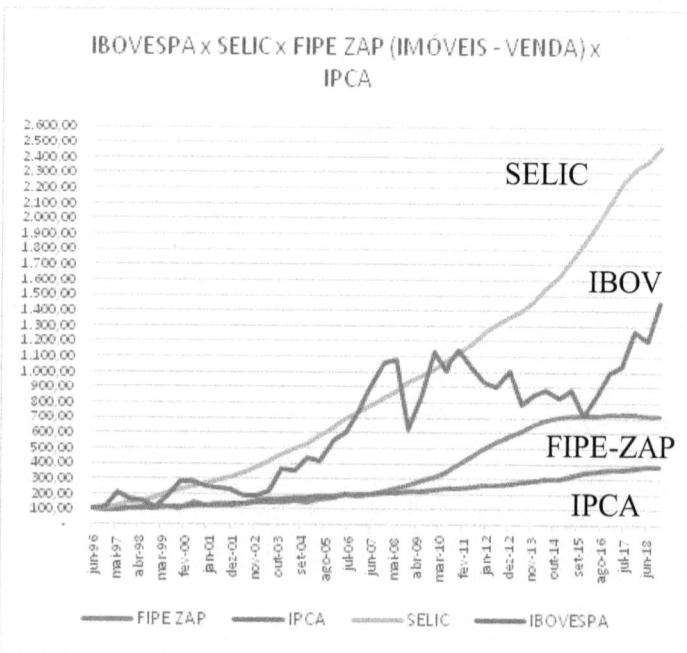

Disregarding the highly inflationary period, prior to 1995, which greatly distorts the indexes shown here, we have that, from 1996 to 2018, the properties appreciated more than 600% (Fipe Zap - Sale index) and the Selic appreciated more than 2,300%. The IBOVESPA appreciated more than 1,350%. Inflation in the period (IPCA) was almost 300%.

From the information in the table at the end, applying R$ 100.00 to properties in Jun/1996, there would be R$ 721.25 after 270 months, that is, an increase of 621.55% in the period, which corresponds to 0.73% per month = $(1 + 6.2155)^{1/270} - 1)$ or 9.18% per year, in continuous capitalization.

If R$ 100.00 were invested in the Selic rate in Jun/1996, there would be R$ 2,467.47 after 270 months, that is, an increase of 2,367.47% in the period, which corresponds to 1.19% am = $(1 + 23.6747)^{1/270} - 1)$ or 15.31% p.y., in continuous capitalization.

If R$ 100.00 were invested in IBOVESPA in Jun/1996, there would be R$ 1,454.14 after 270 months, that is, an appreciation of 1,354.14% in the period, which corresponds to 1.00% per month = $(1 + 13.5414)^{1/270} - 1)$ or 12.63% p.y., in continuous capitalization.

Inflation in the period (IPCA) was 284.71%, which corresponds to 0.50% p.m or 6.17% p.y., in continuous capitalization.

Considering that the profitability of a rented property is on average 0.50% p.m., there would be an extra appreciation of 284.45% in the period = $(1.005^{270} - 1)$.

If the rents received are reinvested in real estate, the total return in the period would be 2,673.98% [= (1 + 6.2155) x (1 + 2.8445) - 1], which would be higher than the Selic rate yield between Jun/1996 and Dec/2018, of 2,367.47% (= 1.19% p.m.).

The historical monthly profitability of an investment in real estate (considering the rent) is, therefore, 1.23% p.m. (= 1.0073 x 1.0050 - 1) or 15.85% p.y., without discounting inflation.

Doing the opposite, to calculate how much on average the monthly profitability of the rent should be to match the historic Selic (2,367.47% a.p. or 1.19% p.m.), we have:

$$(1.0073 \times \text{Rental Factor}) - 1 = 1.19\%$$

$$\text{Rental factor} = 1.0119/1.0073 = 1.0046$$

$$\% \text{ rental} = \text{Rental Factor} - 1 = \mathbf{0.46\% \text{ p.m.}}$$

This percentage is close to that informed throughout the guide, which varies between 0.40% p.m. and 0.50% p.m., depending on the type of property.

What should be called attention is that there is a risk in the real estate market and that the maintenance of a property requires a lot of care and time, but if the property is small, well located, well managed and acquired for the long term, there are good chances to achieve total return at least close to the Selic rate, with this return being enhanced at times when the basic interest rate of the economy is low (which is the case in 2021: Selic = 2.75% p.y.).

The examples given are also useful for those who buy a property to live in, because the rent that is being neglected to pay on another similar property is considered in the investment's cash flow as an income.

In these examples, the specifics of the properties and their regions are not being considered, adopting a national and general index, the payment of taxes on profits and the non-receipt of rents due to default or unemployment.

The monthly rent percentage equal to 0.46% is a necessary average to reach the same Selic variation.

As for IBOVESPA, it would be in 3rd place, with historical monthly appreciation of 1.00% and annual value of 12.63%.

Looking back, in a simple analysis of these data, investment in fixed income linked to Selic would be the best of all, given the practicality of the operation and the low risk.

Taking into account that the Selic is in March 2021 at 2.75% p.y., would it be worth it at that moment to invest in real estate or in variable income, which have a much greater risk?

This is everyone's decision. The Risk x Return of each operation must be evaluated. If the investor is risk averse, stay in fixed income and guarantee your income. If the investor wants to try to earn more, go to the real estate or equity market (financial), but be aware of the risks you are taking.

In the "Guia fácil para operar no mercado financeiro: Teoria das Carteiras"/"Easy guide to operating in the financial market: Theory of Portfolios" (version for now only in the Portuguese language), it is very detailed how to assess risk x return of an asset portfolio. This guide can be found at:

https://www.amazon.com.br/dp/B08ZH54PLG

Appendix 2: ideal historical percentages for an asset portfolio that contains investments in Selic, Dollar, IPCA, Real Estate and Shares

Here will be shown what are the ideal historical percentages for an asset portfolio that contains investments in Selic, Dollar, IPCA, Real Estate and Shares, all with a focus on minimizing the volatility of the portfolio as a whole or maximizing its return.

As stated in the previous annex, in the "Guia fácil para operar no mercado financeiro: Teoria das Carteiras"/"Easy guide to operating in the financial market: Theory of Portfolios" (version for now only in the Portuguese language), it is very detailed how to assess risk x return of an asset portfolio. This guide can be found at:

https://www.amazon.com.br/dp/B08ZH54PLG

It will be seen that if the investor had 40% of his portfolio invested in Selic, 40% invested in IPCA, 16.4% invested in real estate, 1.3% invested in Ibovespa and 2.3% invested in dollars, between Jun/1996 and Dec/2018, it would have obtained a performance with a return of 10.38% p.y. and an optimized (minimized) portfolio volatility (risk) of only 4.08% p.y.

And, if the investor had 40% of his portfolio invested in Selic, 0% invested in IPCA, 42.3% invested in real estate, 6.1% invested in Ibovespa and 11.7% invested in dollars, in the same period, he it would have obtained an optimized (maximized) return of 12.04% p.y., with a portfolio volatility (risk) of 7.95% p.y..

As a comparison, if he had invested in only one of these assets, he would have had the following risk x return ratio between Jun/1996 and Dec/2018:

	Average (p.y.)	Volatility (p.y.)
IPCA	6.1%	2.3%
Selic	15.1%	4.6%
Real Estate	9.5%	10.6%
Dollar	8.0%	20.5%
Ibovespa	18.0%	34.8%

The values in the table differ slightly from those in the previous annex, because in that annex the continuous rate was calculated, based on the initial and final values of each item. In the table, data were obtained using the average of the entire semiannual data history, annualized.

It is customary for someone to talk around or read about finance news so as not to "put the same eggs in the same basket", whether for short or long term investments, because this reduces volatility (risk).

And you can still hear someone say "oh, for the long term, invest, for example, 50% in fixed income, 30% in shares, 10% in real estate funds and 10% in dollars" or "have 40% of your equity invested in real estate, 30% invested in shares and 30% invested in Tesouro Direto IPCA 2035 (government bonds linked to inflation maturing in 2035)" etc, without showing why these values.

So, here, a notion of the historical proportions of each of these assets will be given, according to the assumed risk x return ratio. It will be up to the reader to decide whether or not to apply such percentages to their <u>long-term</u> investments. This is often a very private decision.

The returns and volatilities reported below will not necessarily be repeated, not least because the Selic's long-term estimate is for stabilization, but it will be possible to get a sense of how these assets correlate and how they can vary over time according to the direction of the economy.

To calculate the risk x return of these assets in Excel, using the Markowitz Theory (seen in the "Guia fácil para operar no mercado financeiro: Teoria das Carteiras"/Easy guide to operate in the financial market: Theory of Portfolios"), the data at the end of the annex (semi-annual quotations) are used.

The graph showing the semiannual evolution of the indices between Jun/1996 and Dec/2018 is as follows:

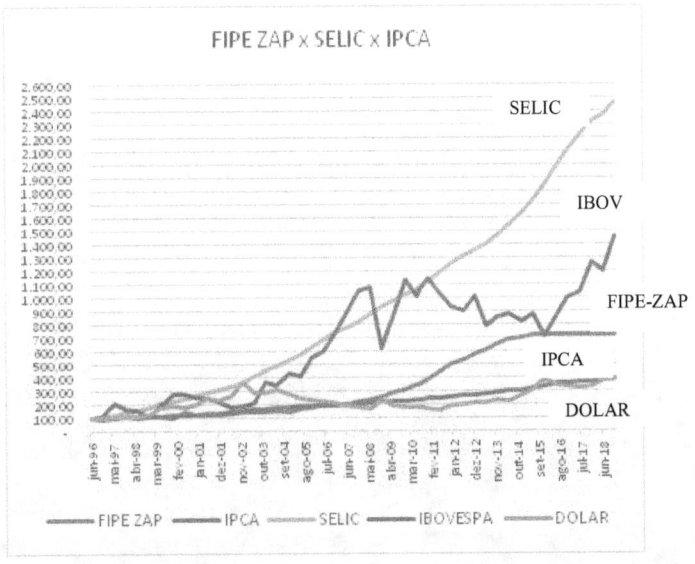

From the graph, for some time, the dollar has practically followed inflation (IPCA) and in 270 months it had practically the same profitability. That's what they say, but no one shows the data.

In order of increasing historical volatility, the portfolios containing percentages of investments in Selic, IPCA, Real Estate (represented by the index Fipe-Zap), Ibovespa and Dollar, with the respective historical returns (between Jun/1996 and Dec/2018) are:

PORTFOLIO	PERCENTAGE IN THE PORTFOLIO					RETURN FROM THE PORTFOLIO (p.y.)	PORTFOLIO RISK (p.y.)	
	SELIC	IPCA	REAL ESTATE	IBOVESPA	DOLLAR			
1	40.0%	40.0%	16.4%	1.3%	2.3%	10.38%	4.08%	(lowest risk)
2	30.0%	40.0%	22.8%	2.6%	4.7%	9.91%	4.59%	
3	40.0%	30.0%	22.9%	2.5%	4.6%	10.80%	4.88%	
4	20.0%	40.0%	29.1%	3.8%	7.1%	9.43%	5.35%	
5	30.0%	30.0%	29.2%	3.8%	7.0%	10.31%	5.56%	
6	40.0%	20.0%	29.3%	3.7%	7.0%	11.22%	5.82%	
7	10.0%	40.0%	35.4%	5.1%	9.5%	8.95%	6.28%	
8	20.0%	30.0%	35.5%	5.0%	9.4%	9.85%	6.40%	
9	30.0%	20.0%	35.7%	4.9%	9.4%	10.73%	6.61%	
10	40.0%	10.0%	35.8%	4.9%	9.3%	11.64%	6.85%	
11	0.0%	40.0%	41.7%	6.4%	11.9%	8.47%	7.31%	
12	10.0%	30.0%	41.9%	6.3%	11.8%	9.37%	7.37%	
13	20.0%	20.0%	42.0%	6.2%	11.8%	10.25%	7.52%	
14	30.0%	10.0%	42.1%	6.1%	11.7%	11.15%	7.70%	
15	40.0%	0.0%	42.3%	6.1%	11.7%	12.04%	7.95%	(greatest return)
16	0.0%	30.0%	48.2%	7.6%	14.2%	8.89%	8.43%	
17	10.0%	20.0%	48.3%	7.5%	14.2%	9.79%	8.51%	
18	20.0%	10.0%	48.5%	7.4%	14.1%	10.67%	8.66%	
19	30.0%	0.0%	48.6%	7.3%	14.1%	11.58%	8.85%	
20	0.0%	20.0%	54.6%	8.8%	16.6%	9.31%	9.60%	
21	10.0%	10.0%	54.8%	8.7%	16.5%	10.19%	9.68%	
22	20.0%	0.0%	54.9%	8.6%	16.5%	11.09%	9.83%	
23	0.0%	10.0%	61.1%	10.0%	18.9%	9.73%	10.78%	
24	10.0%	0.0%	61.2%	9.9%	18.9%	10.61%	10.88%	
25	0.0%	0.0%	67.6%	11.2%	21.2%	10.12%	11.98%	

Based on the table, attention is drawn to the fact that, if analyzed correctly, it will be seen that the lowest risk portfolio will not always have the lowest return. Or that the one with the highest return will have the greatest risk.

See, for example, portfolio 1, with lower risk, with an annual return of 10.38%. There are 14 other portfolios with a higher risk than portfolio 1 and with a lower annual return, using the same assets in different proportions of the total.

Based on the correlations between the returns of each asset, it is possible to optimize the risk x return ratio of the portfolio. The ideal, which is shown in the "Guia fácil para operar no mercado financeiro: Teoria das Carteiras"/"Easy guide to operate in the financial market: Portfolio Theory", is that the correlations between assets are less than 0.7 so that the optimization of the portfolio is efficient. The best is that they are negative.

In conclusion, what the investor will apply from now on (and in what proportion) will depend on how much risk he is prone to take, according to the returns, and on which asset he is betting more at the moment, thinking about the long term. This table can help you in this decision making, to give you an idea of how the indices have varied over time with historical economic situations.

Data used:

	INDEX QUOTATION					Return (per semester – p.s.)				
	REAL ESTATE	IBOVESPA	DOLLAR	IPCA	SELIC	REAL ESTATE	IBOVESPA	DOLLAR	IPCA	SELIC
01/06/1996	100.00	100.00	100.00	100.00	100.00					
01/12/1996	91.67	116.48	103.73	102.82	109.68	-8.33%	16.48%	3.73%	2.82%	9.68%
01/06/1997	96.25	207.95	107.29	107.02	120.99	5.00%	78.53%	3.43%	4.09%	10.31%
01/12/1997	108.09	168.72	111.26	108.19	141.01	12.30%	-18.87%	3.70%	1.09%	16.55%
01/06/1998	104.31	160.13	115.34	110.67	158.23	-3.50%	-5.09%	3.66%	2.29%	12.21%
01/12/1998	108.78	112.25	120.34	109.98	179.78	4.29%	-29.90%	4.34%	0.62%	13.62%
01/06/1999	115.58	192.38	178.65	114.34	207.63	6.25%	71.39%	48.46%	3.96%	15.49%
01/12/1999	105.35	282.80	184.73	119.82	226.19	-8.86%	47.00%	3.40%	4.79%	8.94%
01/06/2000	141.71	276.77	180.52	121.78	247.16	34.52%	-2.13%	-2.28%	1.64%	9.27%
01/12/2000	124.90	252.47	196.49	126.97	266.90	-11.87%	-8.78%	8.84%	4.26%	7.99%
01/06/2001	123.25	240.90	240.43	130.73	286.73	-1.32%	-4.58%	22.37%	2.96%	7.43%
01/12/2001	125.62	224.66	238.04	136.72	312.62	1.92%	-6.74%	-0.99%	4.58%	9.03%
01/06/2002	131.00	184.30	271.40	140.74	339.78	4.28%	-17.96%	14.01%	2.94%	8.69%
01/12/2002	145.55	186.44	372.86	153.85	371.67	11.11%	1.16%	37.38%	9.31%	9.38%
01/06/2003	148.81	214.65	285.27	164.06	415.89	2.24%	15.13%	-23.49%	6.64%	11.90%
01/12/2003	148.81	367.91	292.49	168.16	459.24	0.00%	71.40%	2.53%	2.49%	10.42%
01/06/2004	151.61	349.92	313.33	174.01	493.95	1.89%	-4.89%	7.12%	3.48%	7.56%
01/12/2004	143.15	433.43	274.67	180.94	532.53	-5.58%	23.86%	-12.34%	3.98%	7.81%
01/06/2005	162.38	414.48	244.18	186.65	580.06	13.44%	-4.37%	-11.10%	3.16%	8.92%
01/12/2005	179.91	553.55	229.23	191.23	633.81	10.80%	33.55%	-6.13%	2.45%	9.27%
01/06/2006	197.73	606.08	228.11	194.17	693.55	9.90%	9.49%	-0.49%	1.54%	9.43%
01/12/2006	188.21	735.85	214.38	197.24	741.27	-4.81%	21.41%	-6.02%	1.58%	6.88%
01/06/2007	199.62	899.95	190.68	201.34	783.97	6.06%	22.30%	-11.05%	2.08%	5.76%
01/12/2007	219.25	1,057.03	179.32	206.03	827.90	9.84%	17.45%	-5.96%	2.33%	5.60%

Date								%		
01/06/2008	239.80	1,075.76	163.43	213.54	873.77	9.37%	1.77%	-8.86%	3.64%	5.54%
01/12/2008	260.70	621.29	236.55	218.19	931.50	8.72%	-42.25%	44.73%	2.18%	6.61%
01/06/2009	287.37	851.52	194.29	223.79	979.92	10.23%	37.06%	-17.86%	2.57%	5.20%
01/12/2009	316.96	1,134.83	175.31	227.60	1,02.74	10.30%	33.27%	-9.77%	1.70%	4.37%
01/06/2010	348.21	1,008.22	179.44	234.62	1,066.58	9.86%	-11.16%	2.36%	3.09%	4.29%
01/08/2010	362.01	1,077.86	176.89	234.74	1,07.9.49	3.96%	6.91%	-1.42%	0.05%	1.21%
01/12/2010	393.01	1,146.69	169.63	241.05	1,122.03	8.56%	6.39%	-4.11%	2.69%	3.94%
01/06/2011	448.20	1,032.51	159.36	250.37	1,185.61	14.04%	-9.96%	-6.05%	3.87%	5.67%
01/12/2011	498.96	939.03	185.81	256.72	1,252.66	11.33%	-9.05%	16.60%	2.54%	5.66%
01/06/2012	537.16	899.34	204.12	262.68	1,307.27	7.66%	-4.23%	9.86%	2.32%	4.36%
01/12/2012	577.71	1,008.49	208.09	271.71	1,355.91	7.55%	12.14%	1.94%	3.44%	3.72%
01/06/2013	612.08	785.20	213.35	280.27	1,402.60	5.95%	-22.14%	2.53%	3.15%	3.44%
01/12/2013	658.08	852.21	233.19	287.77	1,468.38	7.51%	8.53%	9.30%	2.68%	4.69%
01/06/2014	687.09	879.70	223.14	298.55	1,543.94	4.41%	3.22%	-4.31%	3.75%	5.15%
01/12/2014	706.33	827.40	266.77	306.21	1,632.38	2.80%	-5.95%	19.56%	2.57%	5.73%
01/06/2015	721.85	878.26	309.90	325.11	1,737.12	2.20%	6.15%	16.17%	6.17%	6.42%
01/12/2015	721.48	717.25	386.45	338.89	1,850.23	-0.05%	-18.33%	24.70%	4.24%	6.51%
01/06/2016	721.77	852.55	347.16	353.86	1,975.77	0.04%	18.86%	-10.17%	4.42%	6.79%
01/12/2016	724.81	996.49	337.79	360.20	2,103.83	0.42%	16.88%	-2.70%	1.79%	6.48%
01/06/2017	725.17	1,040.72	327.87	364.47	2,228.97	0.05%	4.44%	-2.94%	1.18%	5.95%
01/12/2017	723.00	1,264.12	331.26	370.82	2,320.16	-0.30%	21.47%	1.04%	1.74%	4.09%
01/06/2018	721.84	1,203.91	376.81	380.47	2,372.75	-0.16%	-4.76%	13.75%	2.60%	2.27%
01/12/2018	721.55	1,454.14	390.31	384.71	2,467.47	-0.04%	20.79%	3.58%	1.11%	3.99%
average (p.s.)						4.65%	8.61%	3.94%	2.99%	7.27%
standard deviation (p.s.)						7.51%	24.62%	14.47%	1.66%	3.22%

Covariances

	REAL ESTATE	IBOVESPA	DOLLAR	IPCA	SELIC
REAL ESTATE	0.00564	-0.00292	-0.00045	-0.00014	0.00000
IBOVESPA	-0.00292	0.06062	-0.00672	0.00046	0.00126
DOLLAR	-0.00045	-0.00672	0.02094	0.00048	0.00077
IPCA	-0.00014	0.00046	0.00048	0.00028	0.00007
SELIC	0.00000	0.00126	0.00077	0.00007	0.00103

Correlations

	REAL ESTATE	IBOVESPA	DOLLAR	IPCA	SELIC
REAL ESTATE	1.00000	-0.15767	-0.04178	-0.11373	-0.00152
IBOVESPA	-0.15767	1.00000	-0.18861	0.11133	0.15911
DOLLAR	-0.04178	-0.18861	1.00000	0.20133	0.16450
IPCA	-0.11373	0.11133	0.20133	1.00000	0.12975
SELIC	-0.00152	0.15911	0.16450	0.12975	1.00000

Appendix 3: financial analysis of the payment of real estate financing installments with the rent received and whether it is advantageous to finance a property

Here, two subjects will be dealt with, which are interrelated:

1) whether it is advantageous to pay the mortgage installments with the rent received; and

2) whether it is advantageous to finance a property.

The answer is **yes** for both, as long as you invest for the long term and believe that historical returns on real estate will remain, that small properties are privileged, that there is discipline in the payment of installments, that you realize that, on average, the real estate market is of low liquidity, that there is patience and dedication in the administration of rental contracts and, the main thing: **that the Selic remains low in the long term, as the comparatives will be with it**.

These issues have seen and changed appear in news about finance and economics, but no one is sure how the analysis can be done and almost everyone is on the fence about the answer. It will then be attempted to show here with real data and in a very simple way how to make this assessment.

The focus here is mathematical-financial. Therefore, medium and long-term economic projections that change the assumptions can impact on decisions, so the investment conclusion is 100% of each one.

See the example:

Suppose an investor wants to buy a (small) property for R$ 300,000 and has 100% of the money available for that investment plus R$ 90,000 to pay taxes and furnish the property.

If, in the negotiations, the seller does not signal a good discount for the possibility of payment in cash, the investor decides to quote the provision of a real estate financing that covers a certain debt balance.

In order to make the analysis more intuitive, the option of real estate financing through the Price System (with constant installments) and 50% of the property value will be shown here, as this way the provision of financing is somewhere between 0.5% and 0.6 % of the value of the property, that is, the value of the installment is close to the value of the rent receivable (<u>for small properties</u>).

Let's say that, for a simulation on a website of a banking institution, with the purpose of financing a property of R$ 300 thousand through the Price System, the maximum amount that the bank would finance was R$ 150 thousand (50%), the maximum term 20 years and the lowest initial installment was R$ 1,376.50 (CET of 9.68% pa, rate close to the midpoint of recent history). Conservatively, the TR will be considered in the correction of the outstanding balance (historical TR = 2.57% p.y.*) and, thus, the provision of real estate financing would be FIXED at approximately R$ 1,635.00/month, which would correspond to a total effective cost (CET) of 12.50% p.y..

This analysis is still conservative due to the fact that the TR have stayed equal to zero in recent years (ref. 2021), on account of the Selic rate below 8.50% p.y. If these conditions remain so (Selic low), the profitability with properties will be higher, because the **FIXED** installment admitted in the calculations, which considers the historical TR of 2.57% p.y., will actually be R$ 1,376.50, if TR = 0.00% p.y..

The installment of R$ 1,635.00/month corresponds to almost 0.55% of the property's value (R$ 300 thousand).

*On the Bacen website (www.bcb.gov.br), in the citizen's calculator, the TR varied + 77% between Jun/1996 and Dec/2018 (270 months), the period used to check the variations of the properties and Selic to the throughout this guide, which will be used here. This corresponds to 0.20% p.m. or 2.57% p.y. Applying this factor to the CET calculated based on the initial installment, the final CET is 12.50% (= 1, 0968 x 1.0257 –1).

And is it possible to achieve this net monthly profitability of 0.55% with rent?

The answer is **YES**, as long as it is a small property, with a high standard of quality, with a condominium with good infrastructure (swimming pool, gym, sauna etc.) and 24h doorman, well located, with good closets, good furniture and good appliances.

Therefore, the analysis will be based on this type of property and the average net profitability of 0.55% p.m. with rent will be admitted as coherent and real. For larger properties, which rent less than 0.55% p.m., the accounts must be adapted, but it can still be advantageous if the Selic's profitability is lower than its historical value, but with a slightly lower return.

The practical comparisons that will be made are as follows in relation to what yields more in 20 years assuming that historical returns will remain:

1) R$ 150 thousand invested in a property worth R$ 300 thousand, with an extra cost of R$ 45 thousand, financing the other R$ 150 thousand and paying the corresponding installment with the rent received, amortizing the outstanding balance with the surpluses rent, or this R$ 195 thousand (R$ 150 thousand + R$ 45 thousand) invested in Selic?; and

2) of the R$ 390 thousand available, invest R$ 345 thousand in cash in 1 property and invest in Selic the rent and the remaining R$ 45 thousand, or invest R$ 300 thousand in the purchase of 2 properties, with an extra cost of R$ 90 thousand for both, totaling R$ 390 thousand, but entering R$ 300 thousand in both and financing the remaining R$ 300 thousand (2 x R$ 150 thousand), receiving rent and amortizing the outstanding balance with the surpluses of the rent?

Analysis of Question 1):

From the previous annexes, it was shown that between Jun/1996 and Dec/2018 the Selic yielded 15.31% p.y. or 1.19% p.m. and properties (sale + rent) appreciated 15.85% p.y. or 1.23% p.m. If we consider only the sales values, the properties appreciated 9.18% p.y. or 0.73% p.m. The IPCA increased 6.17% p.a. or 0.50% p.m. This is a rental correction index.

For the property, only the R$ 300 thousand are valued (the extra R$ 45 thousand were one-off costs that are not valued over time). In the first month, the rent received of almost R$ 1,635.00 will be used to pay the 1st installment, of the same amount. In this 1st month, the property will increase 0.73% and will be worth R$ 302,190.00. The rent will not change for 12 months, according to the lease agreements, so there will be no surplus of rent in this period in relation to the amount paid in the housing installment. After 12 months, the rent is adjusted for inflation (historical IPCA = 0.5% p.m.). It will be admitted that the contracts last an average of 24 months, then, after the first 12 months, the correction is by the IPCA and, after the next 12 months, the correction is at market value, in a new contract, that is, it applies the 0.55% on the market value of the property and this new rent is adopted for 12 months and so on.

Then, after the first 12 months, the rent will be worth R$ 1,735.36 (= 1635.00 x 1.005^{12}), as it is adjusted by the annual IPCA.

Now there will be R$ 100.81/month after receiving the rent and paying the installment, which is FIXED when we admit the historical TR in your account.

This R$ 100.81 will be used to amortize the outstanding balance over 12 months, until the rent is corrected to the market (as we admit that, on average, the contracts will last for 24 months). Then, every month, an amortization bill of that amount must be issued. And so on, as shown in the table below.

MONTH	PROPERTY VALUE	PAYMENT OF PROPERTY FINANCING PROVISION	CONTRACTUAL INTEREST	CONTRACTUAL AMORTIZATION	GAINS WITH RENT	DIFFERENCE, TO DEBATE DEBT BALANCE (EXTRA AMORTIZATION)	DEBT BALANCE
0	300,000.00						150,000.00
1	302,190.00	R$1,634.54	1,479.54	155.00	1,634.54	-	149,845.00
2	304,395.99	R$1,634.54	1,478.01	156.53	1,634.54	-	149,688.46
(...)	(...)	(...)	(...)	(...)	(...)	(...)	(...)
12	327,361.24	R$1,634.54	1,461.86	172.68	1,634.54	-	148,035.64
13	329,750.98	R$1,634.54	1,460.16	174.38	1,735.36	100.81	147,760.44
14	332,158.16	R$1,633.43	1,457.45	175.98	1,735.36	101.93	147,482.53
(...)	(...)	(...)	(...)	(...)	(...)	(...)	(...)
24	357,217.95	R$1,621.50	1,428.79	192.71	1,735.36	113.86	144,548.12
25	359,825.64	R$1,620.22	1,425.76	194.46	1,946.29	326.07	144,027.59
(...)	(...)	(...)	(...)	(...)	(...)	(...)	(...)
111	676,014.88	R$90.61	65.32	25.29	3,488.49	3,397.88	3,198.68
112	684,419.48	R$43.94	31.55	12.39	3,488.49	3,444.55	-258.26

From the table, after 112 months, the property would be paid and worth R$ 684,419.48 thousand. There would still be R$ 258.26 left. That is, the initial investment of R$ 195 thousand turned this amount. The return is 14.40% p.a., for 112 months. It is a good profitability, but it would not surpass the historic Selic rate, of 15.31% p.y., with low risk, high liquidity and less work. If invested in Selic, the R$ 195 thousand would become R$ 733 thousand after 112 months. Real estate has a historical risk of almost 11% p.y., low liquidity and requires patience in the management of lease agreements.

Analysis of Question 2):

To answer question 2) the same period as the previous analysis in which the property is paid will be considered, that is, 112 months.

If we apply R$ 345 thousand in cash to a property and we want to receive 0.55% p.m. rent to apply it in Selic, and also apply the remaining R$ 45 thousand in Selic, we would have, after 112 months:

- for the property: R$ 684,419.48 (see analysis 1);

- for the R$ 45 thousand in Selic: R$ 169,286.86; and

- for rentals received and applied in Selic: R$ 507,713.40.

Total = R$ 684,419.48 + R$ 169,286.86 + R$ 507,713.40

Total = R$ 1,361,419.71

We saw in analysis 1) that we would have R$ 684,419.48 for 1 property after 112 months, if we financed 50% of its value and used the surplus rent to amortize the debt balance. Therefore, if we had done this with 2 properties, we would have a total final value of **R$ 1,368,838.91** at the end of 112 months under these conditions. It is practically the same amount to pay in cash 1 property and apply rent and extra money (R$ 45 thousand) in Selic.

Conclusion:

Applying R$ 195 thousand in <u>historical</u> Selic, we would have about **R$ 733 thousand** after 112 months (15.31% p.a.). And, applying the same amount to a financed property and using the rent to pay the installments and amortize the outstanding balance "extra", we would have **R$ 684 thousand** (14.40% pa) in that period, if we consider the <u>historical</u> valuation of the properties and the <u>market</u> profitability for rent. In other words, investing in Selic is a little more advantageous than buying financed property and paying the real estate installments with the rent received, assuming historical values.

In another analysis, buying a property of R$ 345 thousand and applying the rents received and another R$ 45 thousand in historic Selic, we would have **R$ 1,361,419.71** after 112 months. And, by applying R$ 390 thousand to the purchase of two financed properties and using the rents to pay the installments and amortize the outstanding balance "extra", we would have **R$ 1,368,838.91** after 112 months. In other words, paying in cash or financing the property results in almost the same thing with the historical values of Selic and real estate.

In magnitude, the returns would be very close in both analyzes, but it is much more practical and safer to apply in Selic than in real estate. However, for the market, Selic signals to stay below 10% p.y. in the long run, which would make investment in real estate more attractive if historical valuations are maintained.

Still, with historical data, the investment in a financed property would have a higher advantage than the Selic if the investor died or became disabled until just before 112 months, as the contractual insurance would prepay the balance due for the good profit of its assets heirs and this would increase profitability and may exceed Selic's profitability. But nobody wants that, right? Just the comment.

If the investor accesses the ANBIMA (Brazilian Association of Financial and Capital Markets Entities) website at www.anbima.com.br/pt_br/informar/curvas-de-juros-fechamento.htm, he can observe the data for the curves DI, forward and spot interest rates.

Or the investor can consult the "Guia fácil para operar no mercado financeiro: Derivativos: Futuros, Termos e Swaps"/"Easy guide to operate in the financial market: Derivatives: Futures, Terms and Swaps" (version for now only in Portuguese) at https://www.amazon.com.br/dp/B08ZC4WJ6V and, based on the adjusted PUs (adjusted Unit Prices of futures contracts), taken from the B3 website, you can assemble the DI (depósito interbancário/interbank deposit rate ≈ Selic), forward and spot curves for analysis on your own.

Of the data consulted in March 2021, the longest contract was that of Jan/2033. For the term of 112 months in relation to March 2021, it would fall in 2030, so the curve covers that period. The maximum DI (interbank deposit rate ≈ Selic) rate was 9.18% p.a., which is in the order of the historical variation of the prices (only) of the properties, by coincidence.

In this case, there would be a "fat" in the investment of real estate that would be the rent received, about 0.5% extra.

For this DI rate, investments in analyzes 1) and 2) would return **R$ 440 thousand** (against R$ 733 thousand) and **R$ 1,175,953.90** (against R$ 1,361,419.71), respectively.

The properties, repeating the values, would be worth for each analysis, respectively, **R$ 684 thousand** and **R$ 1,368,838.91**, considering the historical profitability.

Here, conservatively in the analysis of real estate profitability, the historical TR of 2.57% p.y. in the correction of the debt balance of financing, even if it tends to be lower with the projected Selic lower than the historic Selic.

So, the big questions to make a decision are: will the Selic really not exceed 10% in the long run? Will real estate properties continue to appreciate 0.73% p.m.? Will the investor achieve a net profit with a rent of about 0.55% per week on the value of the property? Will the investor have the discipline to pay the installment of the property? Will the investor have the patience to manage a rental agreement?

These considerations are expected to assist the investor in making a decision.

It is much more practical and safer to apply in Selic historically, but with low rates today (ref. 2021), real estate can be a good opportunity, considering the inventories of developers and prices stabilized for a long time.

Both are very good long-term investments historically, but the decision is up to the investor, because the future nobody foresees and, as with any investment, it is not possible to project real profitability without risk.

The important thing is for the investor to know the risk and the return of each possibility in order to be able to decide whether to enter, remain in or leave an investment.

With a good perception on the part of the investor about the country's macroeconomic scenario, perhaps these choices can be facilitated.

Bibliography

www.melhortaxa.com.br;

www.b3.com.br;

www.caixa.gov.br;

www.airbnb.com.br;

www.booking.com;

www.valorinveste.globo.com;

www.fipezap.zapimoveis.com.br;

www.fipe.org.br/pt-br/indices/fipezap/#fipezap-historico;

www.ibge.gov.br;

www.bcb.gov.br;

www.anbima.com.br;

www.onfly.com.br;

Rissato, Flavio. Guia fácil para operar no mercado financeiro/ Easy guide to operating in the financial market (several volumes, only in Portuguese, for now). 2021. Kindle (www.amazon.com.br).

www.ingramcontent.com/pod-product-compliance
Lightning Source LLC
Chambersburg PA
CBHW050244220526
45465CB00002B/537